WINE-
DARK
SEA

WINE-DARK SEA

NEW & SELECTED POEMS & TRANSLATIONS

SCOTT EDWARD ANDERSON

SHANTI ARTS PUBLISHING
BRUNSWICK, MAINE

WINE-DARK SEA
NEW & SELECTED POEMS & TRANSLATIONS

ℭ

Published by Shanti Arts Publishing
Designed by Shanti Arts Designs

Cover image by Patricia J. Finley, *My Soul Sings*,
2018. Acrylic paint and ink in resin. 36 x 48
inches. Used with permission of the artist.

Shanti Arts LLC
193 Hillside Road
Brunswick, Maine 04011
shantiarts.com

Printed in the United States of America

ISBN: 978-1-956056-26-6 (softcover)

Library of Congress Control Number: 2022931369

for Samantha

F, C & A

Contents

Some Indiscretions

Translations & Variations

from *Fallow Field*

Uncollected Poems

New Poems & Translations

Wine-Dark Sea

Wine-Dark Sea

I

To the retired classicist watching a vivid sunset
at the mouth of Maine's Damariscotta River,
the color of sea resembles Mavrodaphne,
a wine of deep purple-brown hue
made from a black grape indigenous
to the Northern Peloponnesus.
The upper reaches of sky, filled with ash
from the eruption of Mount St. Helens
over 3,000 miles away, cast a deep red
on the outgoing tide, river of many fishes.
Perhaps Homer's "wine-dark sea" is ashy-sunset-red.

ℭ

The phrase "wine-dark" established foothold through Liddell
and Scott's *Greek-English Lexicon* of 1843. Liddell's daughter, of
course, inspired Lewis Carroll's *Alice's Adventures in Wonderland*
(1865). "*Don't drink me,*" the wine-dark sea might say to her,
however much she may be tempted—

Oînops póntos, from *oînos* + *óps*. *Oînos*, meaning wine + *óps*,
meaning face, and *póntos*, meaning sea. So, literally, "wine-face
sea." But what *is* wine-face? Ruddy, flushed, a little bleary-eyed,
after having consumed an entire bottle or two in the gregarious
night—Surely though *óps* can mean "eye" as well as "face." So, is it
the reddish wine-colored whites of the eyes of a night of serious
drinking or the dark-bluish circles of next morning's hangover?

❧

Some theorize the ancient Greeks
could not see the color blue,
their optical palate limited
to black and white, and possibly red.
Such cultural blindness cannot be proved;
their experience of color may have consisted,
rather, of equal parts movement and shimmer—
porphureos, that glimmer effect on sea-surface
when light refracts or reflects
at different hours and in different weathers,
wine's tint recalling the luster of liquid
inside the terracotta cups used to drink it—

❧

Beyond the sea, Homer uses the epithet to describe an ox
(ancestor to Bunyan's Babe the Blue Ox?)—the adjective appears
a dozen times across the *Iliad* and *Odyssey*—and, further, it is
used to describe the eyes of Dionysus, god of winemaking, in
the *Bacchae* of Euripides. (Were *his* eyes blue or made "blue" by
drinking too much wine?)

Still another theory has it the ancient Greeks mixed their wine
with the alkaline freshwaters of the Peloponnesus, which
would have turned their red wine to blue, alkalinity converting
anthocyanins through chemistry, as with a drop of wine on a
white napkin, tablecloth, or bedsheet—

Many believe Homer meant open waters
and stormy seas, rather than coasts, a sea
rough and tossed, its rising crests of deep opacity.
Out on open water, the horizon can cause
a trick of the light when a blood-red sun
dips below the surface, the sky aflame,
until sea and sky are indistinguishable.
A good portent for those at sea:
"Red skies at night, sailor's delight,"
goes the old saying . . .
can the same be said for red seas?

｡

Robert Fitzgerald, whose translation of *The Odyssey* variously
enchanted or bored thousands of high school students since its
first appearance in 1961, once recalled being on board a ship
heading into the Saronic Gulf of the Aegean Sea, and that "the
contrast of the bare arid baked land against the sea, gave the
sea such a richness of hue" he felt as though they were "sailing
through a bowl of dye," the depth of hue was like that of a good
red wine.

Emily Wilson employs "wine-dark" in her *Odyssey* translation,
saying, "Like wine, the sea changes us. Like a face, it seems to see
and reflect." And, elsewhere, "the sea is dark and bubbly, and it's
where no vines grow (fruitless): its *wineface* is an alien mirror of
our cultured human faces . . . a *noface* face, an inhuman eye."

ॐ

Perhaps Homer meant the waters teeming
with blood from Odysseus's shipwreck
at Poseidon's wrath or filled with the tears
wept by Achilles as he looked
toward the wine-dark sea, reaching
for the *oínopa pónton*, the sea-passage
that, despite its danger, provides
a pathway to the longing in his heart: *home*.

II

While those of us stuck at home
during this global pandemic
could only dream of crossing the sea,
whether wine-dark or slate gray,
crews on cruise ships were quarantined
on board for months in cramped quarters
with perhaps one portal window,
and enough room for a bunk bed,
minifridge, and a small desk.
Ghost ships on the wine-dark sea:
crews allowed outside their cabins
at mealtime for perhaps an hour or two—
several committed suicide
after the guests had gone.

During the early days of the pandemic,
cruise ships were an "epidemiological nightmare"
with their potent combination of "prolific
international travel, line dancing,

endless buffets, and indoor karaoke—"
which, even in non-pandemic times,
seems like a toxic nightmare to me.

≈

"On April 29, an electrical engineer from Poland on Royal
Caribbean's Jewel of the Seas disappeared while the ship was
anchored in the Saronic Gulf, south of Athens. Ship security
cameras captured him leaping into the water that morning . . . "
—Austin Carr, Bloomberg Businessweek

Two weeks later, a waitress from Ukraine, jumped to her death
from Carnival's *Regal Princess* overboard somewhere near
Rotterdam. Others hung themselves from doorknobs or balcony
railings aboard their ships—

≈

HOW MANY
MORE
SUICIDES
YOU NEED

—a protest sign on the deck of the *Majesty of the Seas*, May 2020

≈

Auden, in "The Shield of Achilles,"
writes of "ships upon untamed seas"
(I could have sworn he wrote "wine-dark"—)

Reading his poem now, I am reminded of another line
that speaks to the plight of these crews
and, perhaps, of us all:
"They were small
and could not hope for help and no help came . . . "

III

History, from the Greek, ἰστορία,
historia, meaning, "to learn from inquiry,"
and "knowledge acquired by investigation."
Leading me to *história*—story in Portuguese—
which language also renders
the wine-dark sea, thus: *o mar cor de vinho*,
where *cor* is "color," although it resembles
the English word "core," the central or most
important part of something, the Earth's core,
say, or the "core of an issue," the central part
of a fruit, as in Merriam-Webster's definition:
"especially: the papery or leathery carpels
composing the ripened ovary in a pome fruit
(such as an apple) . . . "

But here, the core of the story,
the central part of my *história*,
at least, or what I've learned from inquiry,
is that the ocean-crossing of my great-grandparents,
heading from the Azores to America, is at the core
of my own history, my own story,
that their individual crossings bore fruit
in the form, not only of my later life,
but of a sort of trauma of separation
they both must have felt, leaving

their island, and which may have been passed
down to me, through RNA, rendering
the wine-dark sea, if not the color of wine,
perhaps the core of my own sensibility.

Ribonucleic acid (RNA) is a polymeric molecule
that serves as a messenger, coding and decoding,
regulating and expressing genes,
"sensing and communicating responses
to cellular signals." In other words,
RNA is a storyteller—
The story it tells, then, is that
of "intergenerational *saudades*"
(as my friend Esmeralda Cabral calls it . . .),
which easily overtakes me, like ocean waves,
and which I'm convinced
was passed down to me from my ancestors.

"Yonder, by the ever-brimming goblet's rim,
the warm waves blush like wine," wrote Melville.
And off the bow of the ship was endless sea,
as if the ship was a floating island,
self-contained, its horizon continually
out of reach, as if anything were within reach.
Emerson's "vast spaces of nature . . .
long intervals of time, years, centuries,"
must have seemed vaster still to a girl of fourteen
or a boy who had just completed his nineteenth trip
around the sun, leaving their island home
for the first time, into an unknowable unknown.

IV

"Olho o mar. Olho o céu. Azuis."
   —Pedro da Silveira

Various shades of blue: Azure, Navy, Royal, Persian,
Cobalt, Denim, Maya, Dodger (Brooklyn or LA),
Lapis Lazuli, Iceberg, Skye (or sky?), Egyptian,
Sapphire, Baby, Admiral, Steel, Vivid Cerulean—
More violet blues: Berry, Moody, Havelock, Cornflower,
Chetwode, Indigo, Fuschia; those favoring greener hues:
Eastern, Bondi, Lagoon, Robin's Egg, Fountain, Hippie,
Vista, Smalt, Aero, Stone, Teal; and the grays: Regal, Chathams,
Aegean, Bahama, Bayoux, Blizzard, Pattens, Peacock, Slate,
Spruce . . .

ℭ

The sea is no color at all,
merely a trick of the light,
reflection or refraction.
Perhaps, then, wine-dark
is meant to evoke
depth of darkness
rather than color,
wine-like darkness
rather than red.

Love at Middle Age

Villanesca

Before the cabin door shuts, I check messages.
You forgot your score for "Spanish Dances" on the piano,
left open at the "Villanesca," a piece with pastoral repetitions you
found hard to reproduce. Your rough interpretation reminds me
of your voice and its effect (or its affect).

Headphones on, I listen to Alicia de Larrocha
performing Granados. The program host has a soothing lisp,
enunciating every *syl – la – ble*, like a reporter on NPR. Quoting
from a review, she says De Larrocha's playing speaks to "a
glorious inevitability achieved through immense discipline."

"Can you bring the score to my rehearsal?" you ask
via voice mail, forgetting my flight this afternoon.
Unlike De Larrocha you always forget the score,
ignore signals, struggle to find the right notes, refuse
to face the music of our own inglorious inevitability.

I press delete, choosing not to repeat past mistakes;
at least, for the duration of my flight.

Phase Change

*a change from one state—solid, liquid, or gas—to
another without a change in chemical composition*

Was it my heat or yours that took me
through phase changes to who I am today?
In my fluid state, I could never be contained.
Flowing, yet never satisfied,
reaching for something that mattered,
wanting to be a solid, authentic person
worthy of heat and attention.
I'd reached the freezing point
by then—cold, I was cold and callous
to a point where no one could hold me.

I became frozen in all ways that matter,
constantly breaking my mold
and splintering off in all directions,
not unlike shards of ice that shatter
rather than completely changing states.
Latent heat of fusion or vaporization—
latent fear of transformation,
fear of the unknown, a state of uncertainty.

And then, attracted by your constant heat,
a kind of sublimation occurred,
both physical and psychological.
I skipped phases like stones
on a surface of ice rather than water.
Who I was before that day evaporated away
and became the man I needed to be—
the man you needed me to become.
I moved from one state to another,
and all was deposition over desolation.

Weather

She came on like a storm
is one way of putting it.
And, as if in a hurricane,
I was blown away.
Now, I'm deep in it,
snowbound and gagged.
No, not gagged; she enjoys
that thing I do with my tongue and teeth
as it negotiates weather patterns
on the back of her neck.
And when the heat of my body
gets close to her chilly frame
it's like the fault line
between a high pressure system
and a low—cold north air
clashing with warm southerly
moisture, leading to a strongly
rising nor'easter of pleasure.
Not all weather is inclement,
you just need to know the right
weatherman, and which way
my wind blows. And, if we're lucky,
we will ride out the storm until dawn.

Love at Middle Age

In the moment when our scars kiss
closing the gap between our laps
—mine from double-hernia surgery;
yours from three C-sections—
we become more aware
of the vicissitudes of beauty,
the latitudes of love,
and gravity of longevity,
than ever in our lives.
And perhaps those other, unseen
scars we share from our lives apart
bind us together.

Summer Love

The female cecropia moth,
Hyalophora cecropia, emerges
as in a stop-action film: swollen
abdomen shrinking while wings
rise, fill, and form. Pheromones
kick in, attracting a male from miles away.
They couple quickly—how easy love can be.
Linked like this, at terminus,
they are most vulnerable to predators.
They will stay this way, available
to each other, for hours—

Under the Linden's Spell

Honey and lemon-peel scent
of the linden tree's pale-yellow flowers
in drooping cymes, late June in the air—
early summer of Brooklyn,
early summer of our love.

We breathed in air rich with its flower's
scent, mingled with our own of lovers spent,
our trunks entwined like Baucis and Philemon—
my oak to your basswood—abundance overflowing,
as we drank from Mercury's Pitcher.

Firehorse

Three summers he tried to break that horse
Longeing her, riding her bareback,
unsaddled and unbridled,
even tried gentling her.
But she just couldn't stop breaking
the rules of their engagement,
couldn't stem the fire of impulse
within her. "Firehorse," he called her,
and kept at her, pulling at her fiery mane,
strapping her with his crop,
even tried biting the back of her neck,
as they said was done by Spanish horsemen.
Still she struggled against the reins,
until he nearly gave up, set her free,
or gave her up to ride another—

Then one day, without sign
or symbol, in a distinct moment
he could feel a change in her movement.
It was palpable. She stopped
in her step, yielding to him,
but not giving up her fire within,
impulse becoming intention.
As if she now understood
his rules were meant not
to control her, but rather
to open her to possibility,
where horse and rider become one.

A Longing Found

Too long I lived in darkness,
a shadow man living a shadow life.
Now I want a real love.
A longing found after too long
looking in all the wrong places.
I want one authentic heart
speaking to me, revealing
secrets inside of me.
She who, when I touch her,
opens to me in a way that only she can.
And I respond as if playing
a musical instrument
I have always known how to play.

Places for a Brief Time Mine

Village, Batanta Island

To the young girl staring at me,
in a village on the island
of Batanta, I have an amusing,
open face; my big eyes,
skin paler than her experience.
I catch her looking at me.
She turns, giggles, whispers
to her friend. Funny gringo
in Ex Officio.

About twenty, twenty-five kids,
crowd around us; all under the age
of ten, most under five.
They pose for pictures
with our digital cameras.
Their scrubbed faces and hand-washed
clothes make neat subjects.
They giggle at the pictures
captured on the viewing screens;
tuck in a stray hair or shirt,
teasing each other.

A long, driftwood fence
lines each side of the one path
through the village. Whitewashed
church, houses with careful,
ornate carvings on the facades.
Neat rows of houses with neat
rows of cassava planted out back,
mango trees and papaya; sand
as white as those houses.

The villagers eat fresh-caught fish
from the sea behind their houses.
One of the men says they must now
go further out each day to find a good catch.
How many people can such a village
support before reaching its limit?
One of my companions,
a businessman from Jakarta,
quickly answers, "One thousand."

—One thousand. What happens then?
He does not answer; I too am silenced.
Now he turns to the children,
speaks in bahasa Indonesian,
steadies to take another picture.

Ten yards away,
by a thatch-roofed house,
stands another girl,
not more than sixteen,
laundry tub at her hip:
already she is pregnant.

A Pantoum for Aceh

Think of the world turned upside down,
The boat on the mud simulating the sea.
The wave beating down on the coast was brown.
Two-hundred thousand swept into the sea.

The boat on the mud simulating the sea;
Remember the baby doll rising out of the flood.
Two-hundred thousand swept into the sea.
The mosque, still standing, is covered in mud.

Remember the baby doll rising out of the flood?
Think of the houses, each righted by mercy;
The mosque, still standing, is cleaned of its mud.
Can you ever get dry after soaking in sea?

Think of the houses, each righted by mercy;
Building back better, lifted up from the ground.
Can you ever get dry after soaking in sea?
Rebuilding a land that was altered and drowned.

Building back better, lifted up from the ground.
The wave beating down on the coast was brown.
Rebuilding a land that was altered and drowned:
Think of the world turned upside down.

Rice Paddies, Rain

NEAR BOGOR, INDONESIA

Monsoon rains fill rice paddies
like a child fills a teacup,
water quickly rushing in, almost overflowing.

The lightening sky seems artificial,
so vivid and sharp the greens,
flat gray mist overlay.

Now the rain is swift and heavy,
impossible-to-stand-in rain,
and as quickly ceasing.

Soil begins to soak-up the water
as we walk out to the prayer house,
step inside before rain returns.

The paddies, *sawah* in bahasa Indonesian,
are empty of rice. They hold;
neither overflowing nor bursting.

Now another pulse of rain,
Five, maybe seven minutes long—
None of the paddies crest.

Perfect water-filled teacup steps
Leading down into the valley—
These farmers *know* rain.

Prayer House

After 150 years, the men took apart
the prayer house one beam, one post at a time
in predictable sequence, stacked
and loaded on two large, heavy trucks,
drove overnight from Kudus to Tapos
—from central to western Java—
to a hill an hour or so south of Jakarta.

Kudus was founded by Sunan Kudus,
who is said to have built the *masjid* there
using doors from the palace of Majapahit,
last of the great Hindu empires
on Malay Archipelago.

Once in Tapos, the men reclaimed
the form of prayer house, beam on post
on beam, and into which we now enter,
first removing shoes and leaving them
where rain thrums, outside the door.
Out the window, greens and browns
of fields and *sawah* made sharper
by heavy rains. Everything breathes life,
even the posts and beams come alive.
Inside, a feeling of intimacy with a God
not my own, but in a way not unfamiliar—

Teak posts are intricately hand-carved
from deep within some deep forest;
ornate scroll work on the beams,
pay homage to a God some say
made the forest from which these posts,
these beams were tooled—

How many things in our lives are borrowed
or built on the past? Even our stories
are crafted from earth and trees, stones
and water, carved old wood, memories and faith.

And we are never alone, not even in our prayers—

—for Roger & Etty Machmud

Peace on Mt. Zion

Peace is such an abstract word,
made concrete by the story
of an Arab shepherd and a Jewish father
told by a guide overlooking
Sultan's Pool, outside the old city
of Jerusalem, from Amichai's poem
about searching for a goat
and a child on Mt. Zion.
Their "temporary failure"
strikes me first, a lasting impression
lingering over the ramparts of the old city
—cradle and shelter of all origins.

So much begins searching
for a goat and a child on a mountain—
new religions, sacrifices, whole
cloths to cover the void,
until the child is found and the goat,
hiding together among the bushes.
The father and the shepherd
cry together and laugh,
and for a moment, all is quiet,
except for their voices,
which you can still hear
echoing over centuries of stone.

    —for Erica

Sirens Rising

ISLA CAPRI, ITALIA

*"O wretched man that I am! Who shall deliver me
from the body of this death?"* (Romans 7:24)

I

Like Tiberius I'm torn
between the flesh & its blood.
Like him, too, I'm of this island's
dark side facing the sea.
You can languish here, succumb
to the madness this island provokes,
or you can flee, denying
your venereal appetite.
Night after night, I give in
to the relentless lure of Pan.
The raucous Neapolitan song
calls to me, instructing my lust,
filling my ears with its chaos.
I am full of life, full of *limoncello*;
blood hurries through my veins,
as if it had some destination—
beyond circulation.

I chase the Roman beauties:
sloe-eyed enchantresses
with slate-black hair and aquiline noses
and arched brows of *la seduttrice*.
Their spry and conclusive limbs
stretch from capricious figures
—they are entanglers.
I may as well be on all fours,
as I creep from taverna to piazzetta.

Together, we fall to my bed,
oozing sweat: couple, come away,
con amorosa cura.
We are sargassum
drifting in a pelagic daze.
In the wretched heat,
the moon is as still and cold
as a marble floor.

II

Sister Serafina,
the unassuming saint of this island,
once induced the prince of darkness
into an adoration of the Savior.
With me, her task is doubly difficult, I'm afraid.
She tries to inveigle me to the Grotta Azzurra
—that knife-wound across the ribs
of Capri's beguiling torso—
for she knows the blue grotto yields up
not the *bagno* where Tiberius
cooled his erotic fires,
nor the relentless lust of legend,
but the Madonna's bluest robes
—the color of sanctity.

It's too late.
I've already gone over the edge,
like the Bishop of Bampopo,
I turn a chaste eye to murder
and drink the sweat of my lovers
in an evaporating recline.
"How shall that come out of man

which was never in him?" the Bishop proffered.
I defile the flowers of Capri,
and search for the power of wild beasts,
deep within the grottoes, dank with sea-wrack.
The dizzy swirl of heaving breath echoes
from every corner of the cyanic cavern.
"*Sono io, sono io*," they claim.
"*Sono io!*"
The Sirens respond to the cry:
"We will succor your willfulness."
"We will cater to your whim—"
Once again, I go to them,
into the depths of an endless night.
They lure me with their dancing
as exquisite as their song
—daughters of Terpsichore!

III

Within sight of Vesuvius,
I follow the trail of obscure desire,
rounding the mealy stone groin
of Arco Naturale. I grow fins,
am lost.
Atop the Salto di Tiberio
and his Villa Jovis,
Tiberius revels in my plight.
He is the dragon of Capri,
whose fiery breath still infects the island.
I see, as if for the first time,
the island's bone-white prominence,
rising above the loam-dark sea.
Grey-pink tufa crags, white limestone,

tender mauve reflexes
upthrusted in pulpy stillness.

And I am born of salt
scorched from the sea's clutch;
the scirocco dashes the island
with its dry spite.
Born of desire,
I return to desire—
The heat
renders my body viscous,
my skin a rubbery porpoise-armor.
I leap from the sea
to plunge to its depths;
the Sirens guide me down
like pilot fish.
I am blessed by their bodies' charms,
their sea-feathers slicked back
by my expert tongue, their breasts
rouged the color of pomegranates
from my rough beard.
"Possess these shores," they whisper.
It's more likely they'll possess me
the Sirens,
in their pagan trinity:
Persuader, Brightface, Bewitcher.

IV

The piazza is a droning blur
at this hour.
The handsome waiters are busy trafficking
caponata and *spaghettini alla puttanesca.*
Women are smoothing their dresses and reapplying
lipstick and rouge, between sips
of dry gin with lemons.
The brackish aroma of homemade wines
and barrels of oil-cured olives,
mingles with the tourists' perfume,
which trickles down their salty cleavage
—intoxicating mist!
I am seated, most nights,
at the table nearest the bar.
It's the closest thing
I've had to home.
This place for a brief time mine.
Leviathan among the Siren victors
—my life, their spoil.

      —for Francesco Durante & Alessandra Carola

Two Poems after Titian's *Metamorphosis*

Diana after the Hunt

Twin paintings, really,
Titian's "Diana and Actaeon"
and the one depicting his death.
Look at the positioning:
in the former, Actaeon, poised
to the left, arm raised parting
the curtain, feet apart, all
broad shouldered and startled.
Diana, on the right,
reclining as an Odalisque,
her right arm raised, one foot
being caressed by a handmaiden,
the other dangling floorward.
Seer and seen, searing gaze
and startled, glance agape.

In the latter, roles are
reversed: Diana to the left,
huntress—bow flexed and ready to shoot,
arrow sharp as her withering glare.
Actaeon, already begun his metamorphosis,
stag's head, toppling and startled still.
This time not by beauty, rather
by the horror of his own dogs
ripping at his unrecognizable flesh.
Look how his upreaching arm
mimics Diana's in its twin,
handmaidens become hounds,
the cadence of his weakness

coming down with the heaviness
of his antler rack, head-heavy
all forgotten heedlessness,
beauty turned bestial:
"If looks could kill . . . "

Actaeon's Words for Diana

Your body from another
era's aesthetic—the curve
of your high hips, soft
roundness of your belly,
the way your breasts swell
in their fullness, open line
of your thighs, slendering down
to shapely, tapered legs.

The dogs of my desire consume
me, torn apart by what I cannot
ever leave behind in the woods,
never give up for the other maidens
near or far—my metamorphosis
is as a lover with an open heart
and an ever-yearning desire for you.
Dogs be damned!

Cândido Rondon Remembering
Teddy Roosevelt

several years after the Roosevelt-Rondon Expedition of 1913–14

When Roosevelt joined our expedition to explore
the River of Doubt from its headwaters to the Amazon,
I had my doubts about him, too, despite
his reputation as a rugged conservationist.

He seemed frailer than expected.
When he got cut on a rock
securing two boats in the rapids,
it took him down swiftly.

He became feverish and delirious, endlessly repeating
    "In Xanadu did Kubla Khan . . . "
As if his own pleasure-dome was there
on the edge of some sunless sea.

Then his son Kermit and our physician told me
Roosevelt still had a bullet lodged in his chest.
He'd been shot while making a speech months back—
spoke for 90 minutes. He never complained.

Our heavy dugout canoes no match
for the river's rapids and rocks,
we lost time with every lost boat.
Still, we drove on, determined.

He insisted I call him *Teodoro*,
as "Roosevelt" was difficult
for my Brazilian tongue.
We feared his loss every day.

When we made it to the confluence,
he asked to be roused and positioned
so as to see the Amazon with his own eyes,
so there could be no more doubt.

We renamed Rio da Dúvida
after him: "Rio Roosevelt."
Although, to me, it will always be
                            Rio *Teodoro*.

Some Birds & Beasts

Owl in the Gloaming

Although real birders frown on it,
I play back songs of birds
trying to lure them out of the wood:
"scree-chee-chee" of song sparrow,
mashing notes of catbird, *"what-cheer,*
what-cheer, what-cheer" of cardinal.

This irritates the birds.
They fly reconnaissance
over my head. Catbird looping
furtive patterns above me,
crossing the path from tree to tree.

Sparrow chasing catbird,
thinking he's got too close,
although the interloper was me
in the unquiet afternoon
sloughing into evening.

Now, a monotonous trill,
tremulous horse-whinny
of the screech owl—
unmistakable, hideous laughter.
Then, overhead, something large,
gray, all wing beat and bodily hum.

All other birds go silent,
in the owl's shadow.
Hidden in the trees,
his scaly, bark-like feathers,
can't be made out in the gloaming.

Now there's a distant thrumming,
not from the bird app on my phone.
Rather, from within my chest,
vibrating on this turning earth,
under an owl's wing.

—for Elizabeth & Walker

Ant Logic

There's an ant crawling inside my tent ceiling,
meaning upside down on the fabric,
perhaps trying to find a way out.

Tiny feelers touching down in front of him,
to no effect; at least, it doesn't seem to help
navigate the cool, white nylon surface.

Yet, I've seen leaf-cutter ants in Ecuadorean
forests appear to know exactly where they are
and where they are going, even how long to get there.

Once I found an unusual ant during a breakfast
at a conference in Aspen. E. O. Wilson,
the renowned myrmecologist, sat at another table.

I took the specimen to him, asking,
"Dr. Wilson, what kind of ant is this?"
He looked at me and then to the ant, saying, *"Lost."*

Doubting Finches

The house finch nest in my porch light
has a curious architecture,
made entirely of found things:
dried seed heads from last year's columbine,
dusky strands of my daughter's hair,
small sticks, rose thorns, bits of string,
a gold thread from a cigarette pack wrapper.
Inside, wool-lined, cotton and fleece,
it holds three eggs, blue with tawny flecks.
The female finch sits on the nest
for an unusually long time; so long,
I fear she is mistaken or my messing
with the nest has disrupted gestation.
She picked her mate for the redness
of his head and chest, proxy for feeding prowess.
(I guess.)

In a few weeks all will be gone:
cherry blossoms drifting on air,
dogwoods blooming, oaks leafing out,
and the female finch finding another mate,
to start a second family this season.
Who was it that said, "Doubt is a privilege
of the faithful"? At least, I think someone
said it or should have. Then it was me,
me finding another mate, another home,
another reason. And I saw they swept out
the finch nest from that old porch light
as soon as I was gone.

The Pre-dawn Song
of the Pearly-eyed Thrasher

Margarops fuscatus

What are you searching for, morning visitor?
A scrap of fruit or nut, an avocado or an orange
to peck into like the egg of some competitor—

Or perhaps you are looking,
with your pearlescent eye,
for some kind of friendship—

Friendship with a kindred spirit,
one who sees, like you do, there are dangers
out there, dangers and uncertainty.

Someone who knows, as you do, survival
depends upon pursuing what you want
without regrets, but with grace and humility.

That, along with a gift for mimicry
and choices based upon trust relationships,
will help you get ahead in this world, my friend.

Or do you seek simply another being who understands
the true meaning of your pre-dawn song's *"eeuu"*
—and doesn't mind its melodious monotony:

I am, I am, I am.

Color or Its Absence: A Birdsong

"Old Sam Peabody Peabody,"
 sings the white-throated sparrow,
 who should really be called
"velvet-throated," this morning,
 his mournful notes anything but pale.
 Is white the absence of color?

Additive color theorists believe
 white is a color because color is light
 and thus reflects all visible colors.
Of course we're talking about timbre
 when we talk about color in song, tone quality.
 Here again, white isn't quite accurate:

white is more noise than song.
 This white-throated fellow, however,
 greeting morning, sounds like he is singing,
"Who wears short-shorts," coloring
 his song an entirely different hue,
 making you blush and me smile.

Lost Art

Lost Art

So rare these days to find
a firm handshake, one with purpose
and power, yet grace and graciousness.
Hand coming at you like a plank,
straight, forward-thinking, un-
self-conscious. You feel it
before you touch: this person means
business, takes you seriously,
acknowledges your presence
and value in the world. What used
to be called Respect.
The opposite is notable too:
flabby fish glad-handed over to you
by a false-friend or the half-shake
with its wimpy wink,
hand not fully extended or open
resulting in a missed opportunity,
like a diver hitting the pool just off-
center, not being able to read the man
behind the hand. Sometimes it's not
about the *feel* of the handshake,
rather what isn't felt—an absence
that shouts, "Disingenuous!"
at best or at least, feigned indifference.
Perhaps that's why, of all the lost arts,
handwritten letters, well-tied ties,
civil discourse, decent air travel,
moderate Republicanism,
I miss the handshake most.
And why, watching a buffoon
performing the clean and jerk

as a greeting to every head of state
and cabinet nominee, I turn
to another lost art and make myself
a proper gin martini:
bone dry, very, very cold,
three olives, shaken not stirred.

    —for Max

Sartorial Advice

A stitch in time saves $9.50, but only if you skip the tailor.
Some say a man is made by nine tailors;
others insist it's the clothes that make the man.
Either way, you should definitely cut your coat
to suit your cloth or, rather, cut your cloth to suit
your coat or—if truth be told—cut your coat-cloth
to the proper dimensions of your suit,
for which a good tailor, if not nine, comes in handy.
(Believe me, I've got a nice bespoke suit made for me
by Martin Greenfield and it suits me just fine.)

Remember that handsome is as handsome does.
So don't wash your dirty linen in public.
Although hanging it out to dry is an option,
especially if you want to save on electricity
or you're concerned about global warming.
Finally, if the shoe fits, wear it, and if it is made of fine
Italian leather, you'll put your best foot forward every time.
I mean, just because the cobbler always wears the worst shoes
and his son goes barefoot, it doesn't mean *you* should.

    —for Robert Pinsky

Calculated Risk

There's evidence accounting goes back to the days
of Mesopotamia, bookkeeping to ancient Iran,
even audits conducted by Egyptians and Babylonians.
Of course, Romans perfected rendering unto Caesar;
while the Brits made accounting a profession.

Computare is the numbers game,
compter is the one who counts.
An accountant reckons by calculation
and settles one's accounts.

Accountancy is for neither faint of heart
nor eye; although the accounting firm
that accounts for my day job
doesn't see fit to supply eye insurance.

Somehow, this doesn't add up to me.
I mean, wouldn't you want to insure
the one thing making sure all the numbers compute?
Alas, just as there's no accounting for taste,
there's no counting on such things as common sense.

App to the Stars

I can't see the stars tonight
in cloud-cover and city night glare.
So I double-tap on my night sky app
make missing stars revealed.

Virgo hiding behind the corner
of the apartment building;
illuminated, first in outline,
then sketched in white-on-black:
woman holding back nothing,
at least until she fades from view.

Moving my iPhone to the left
aiming just below horizon,
the Moon appears, unrisen.
Swinging my view to the apartment
above, Ursa Major hangs, looming.

Back down from ceiling to floor,
I see the sun, a good eight hours away.
Man, there's a lot of space junk up there:
rocket bodies and satellites.

But it's a series of random names
and numbers—a cypher, a type of code,
indicating stars we've shared our universe
with for eons, fascinates me most:
NGC5466, KRAZ, PCEN, 17CRT.

Now panning with my phone facing me,
spinning around and around the room
swinging away, from start to star—
dizzying with every swipe, every turn.
My head full of stars, planets, galaxies.

—in memory of David Simpson, 1952–2015

Philtrum

What do you call
that space between nose and upper lip?
I can never remember.
You know the one: it provides pause
in a mustache, sluice for a runny nose,
u-shaped divot for a kissable upper lip,
point of departure for two sides of a smile.
The name of it always slips my mind.
Is it fulcrum, spatula, petula?
Any of those would suit.
On some faces it's barely there,
not even a hint. On others,
it's a crowning figure,
providing such strong definition
to the mouth as to render significance.
A dimple in some or fat protuberance,
even a deep groove, as if sculpted.
So much variation in the human face.
Is it where facial tics go to rest
or where they begin?
Vestigial medial cleft, useless
to us now or seemingly so.
A term of endearment should suffice
or something Latinate, evoking
historic myth—secula, oridissey, phatama.
No matter, it's there,
perhaps unnamed,
unnameable, even,
or just so ordinary as to go
unnoticed, most of the time.

Some Indiscretions

Forgotten First

I don't even remember her name.
Is that terrible or beautiful?
I don't know.
She was older than me, maybe four years.
I wasn't her first.

The way she took my hand
and ran it along her breasts,
as she brushed my hair
with her fingers, calmed me down.
She was gentle, even loving.
And when she saw or felt my jeans
she was clearly pleased.
When my zipper stuck,
she was careful even with that.

Over as quickly
as she touched me with her lips.
She smiled, wiped her chin,
said, "It's okay,
it happens the first time,"
that I'd learn control.
We could practice, she said,
holding back, if I'd like.
She kissed me on the lips;
hers tasted of salt.

I didn't feel dirty.
She made me feel whole.
You're such a man, she said,
tousling my hair.
I never saw her again.
We moved 400 miles away,
where I would celebrate
my 12th birthday come fall.

A Personal History of Violence

I only lost two fights in my youth.
The first, age 13; his name was Tom.
He said a girl I liked was flat-chested.
True, but I hated him saying it.
He had a long thumbnail that caught me
on the eyelid, blood and sweat
pooled together so I couldn't see.
We wrestled to the ground and I conceded.

The other, a year or two later;
my father, my opponent, was pissed
in both senses, as often the case.
He caught me sneaking out to a concert
he'd forbidden me to attend.
He made me tear up the tickets,
after nearly putting my head
through the living room wall.

The last fight I ever had in school,
I'd overreacted, perennial hothead,
almost made a junior classmate one with a locker,
grip closing in on his throat.
Then I heard my brother's voice or my memory of it,
"Dad, what are you doing?! Dad?!"
And I let go, smoothed my classmate's shirt,
walked away—

Crusoe's Baby Goat

I tell you he did terrible things to me:
dyed my hair all sorts of berry-colors,
pulled my baby goat's beard and *baaa'd*
in my face; his breath was something awful.
He called me names, a different one every day,
and tried to have his way with me,
even offered me to his friend called Friday.
One day they chased me to a cliff's edge
so that I had to jump off—
and land on a craggy rock below,
He wailed and cried, thinking
he'd done it this time, pushed me
over the edge and down to my death.
He didn't know goats!
When they finally left the island,
I was relieved. Good riddance.
And I went back to living
life among my own once again
among our own uninteresting lumber.

    —after Elizabeth Bishop

For T—

I asked her to dance at a black-tie dinner for Literacy.
She said she didn't dance; I'd have to teach her.
Her friend, sitting next seat over, who later played
Hagrid in the Harry Potter films, cautioned,
"Be gentle with her now or you'll be answering to me."

She smiled when I bowed before taking her hand.
She was light on her feet and let me lead.
No one had moved her that way before,
"So in control," she whispered in my ear.
And when the dance was over, I bowed again.

She thanked me, asked did I want to come
see her in "Hamlet" on Broadway? I did.
I brought flowers, met her backstage;
she came out with me; later, I put her in a cab.
"Do you fancy coming uptown?"

I demurred, made some excuse.
Perhaps another time, I suggested,
knowing there would be none.
(I'd no business being there in the first:
I was married; unhappily, but still.)

It couldn't have ended well. No doubt,
we would divorce after a few violent years.
She moving-on to stage and screen;
me, the scapegoat in the press,
spilling popcorn on myself in the house seats.

Letting the House Go

I can't get back to the yellow clapboard house
surrounded by green—maples and oaks in leaf,
fields of peas, berries, and milkweed
leading down to Sunset Lake,
where the two Gladyses, Taylor and Morrill,
taught the town girls to swim.
My father had a chance to buy the house
at some point, but didn't—Gladys Taylor
told me this in a letter I can no longer find.

The little orange-yellow "Pegman" keeps bouncing back above
out of Google Maps street view into aerial ballet.
"The old Fullam house," she called it in a memoir
for the Brookfield Historical Society.
Until my fifties it was the one place I thought of as home,
although it was never my home. When was I last there—
eight or nine years old? Once, in the 90s,
I drove across Brookfield's floating bridge
looking for the road, the house, the path to the lake.

Now I have my own yellow clapboard house,
a place that finally feels like home
and, perhaps, I can let that other house go,
let it become someone else's home.
Gladys Taylor has been dead thirty years,
her companion, the other Gladys, nearly as long;
those Vermont summers a Super 8 color haze.
Memories trapped like fireflies in a jar
with the lid screwed on too tight—

Deaths of the Poets

Sweet sorrow then, when poets die,
as so many of them have this year.
Goodbye to them, as we linger
over their works, forgiving their deeds,
maleficent or magnanimous.
We remember their kind gestures,
wholesome smiles, constructive criticism,
and witty remarks over drinks or dinner.

We seldom recall what a bore they were at readings,
droning on about their poems or rushing through them,
or how they showed up ill-prepared,
rifling through papers trying to find
the exact poem they wanted to read next
or constantly looking at their watch
and asking the host or hostess,
"How much time do I have?"

Sometimes when I hear poets read in their "poet voice,"
I want to shout out "Free Bird," like hecklers at old
rock concerts. "Play 'Free Bird'!" 'til they recite,
"If I leave here tomorrow
Would you still remember me?
For I must be traveling on, now
'Cause there's too many places
I've got to see."

Sweet sorrow in their passing then,
poets gone this year and last and yet to come.
And in our mourning let us not forget
Seamus Heaney's story about two Scottish poets
at a reading, one on the podium struggling
to find his poems and the other, seated in the front row,
saying, "When they said he was going to read,
I thought they meant read *out loud* ..."

Translations & Variations

(translations from Portuguese by Scott Edward Anderson)

Tobacco Shop

I am nothing.
I'll never be more than nothing.
I cannot wish to be more than nothing.
Apart from this, within me are all the dreams of the world.

Windows in my room,
From my room, one of the millions in the world, that no one knows
(And if they knew who I am, what would they know?),
You open to the mystery of a street constantly crossed by people,
To a street inaccessible to all thoughts,
Real, impossibly real; right, unknowingly right,
With the mystery of things beneath the stones and beings,
With death putting moisture on the walls and white hair on men,
With Destiny driving the wagon all the way down the road of nothing.

I'm defeated today, like I know the truth.
I'm lucid today, like I'm about to die,
And feeling no more brotherhood with things
If not a farewell, this house and this side of the street becomes
A row of train carriages, and a whistled departure
From inside my head,
And a jolt of my nerves and a creaking of bones as it leaves.

I'm perplexed today, like one who thought and found and forgot.
I'm torn today, between the loyalty I owe
To the Tobacconist's across the street, something real on the outside,
And the feeling that everything is a dream, something real on the inside.

I failed at everything.

Because I had no purpose, perhaps it was nothing.
The education they gave me,
I left it as through the back window of the house,
I went to the field with great purpose.
But there I found only herbs and trees,
And when there were people, they were the same as the others.
Away from the window, I sit in a chair. What will I think about?

How do I know what I'm going to be, I who don't know what I am?
Be what I think? But I think there's so much!
And there are so many who think of the same thing—there can't
     be so many!
Genius? Currently,
One hundred thousand minds are dreaming they are geniuses like me,
And will history remember any of them, who knows?
Neither will there be manure from so many future achievements.
No, I don't believe in myself.
In every madhouse there are crazy people with so many certainties!
I, who am not sure at all, am I more certain or less certain?
No, not even me . . .
In how many attics and basements of the world
Are there, at this hour, geniuses-to-themselves dreaming?
How many high and noble and lucid aspirations—
Yes, truly, high and noble and lucid—
And who knows if they are achievable,
Will they never see the light of day or reach people's ears?
The world is made for those born to conquer it,
And not for those who dream they can conquer it, even if they're right.
I've dreamed more than what Napoleon achieved.
I have pressed more humanity than Christ to my hypothetical breast,
I've conceived secret philosophies that no Kant has written.
But I am, and perhaps I may always be, the one in the attic,
Although I don't live in it.

I'll always be *the one who wasn't born for this.*
I'll always be *the one who had qualities.*
I'll always be the one who waited for you to open the door of a
        wall without a door
And sang the song of Infinity in a henhouse,
And heard God's voice in a covered well.

Believe in myself? No, not at all.
Pour Nature over my burning head
Your sun, your rain, the wind that combs my hair,
And the rest will come if it comes, or must come, or doesn't.
Slaves of the heart's stars,
We conquered the entire world before getting out of bed.
But we woke up and it's opaque,
We got up and it's rubbed-out,
We left home and it is the whole earth,
Plus the solar system and the Milky Way and the Undefined.

(Eat chocolates, little one;
Eat chocolates!
Look, there's nothing more metaphysical in the world than chocolates.
Look, all religions teach nothing more than confectionery.
Eat, dirty little one, eat!
Would that I could eat chocolates with the same truth with which you eat!
But I think and when I take out the silver paper, which is tin foil,
I throw everything on the floor, as I've thrown out my life.)

But at least it stays the bitterness of what I will never be
The rapid handwriting of these verses,
Broken portico for the Impossible.

But at least I dedicate myself to contempt without tears,
Noble at least in the broad gesture with which I shoot
The dirty clothes that I am, without a list, for the course of things,

And I stay home shirtless.

(You, who console, who doesn't exist and therefore consoles,
Or Greek goddess, conceived as statue but that came alive,
Or Roman patrician, impossibly noble and nefarious,
Or princess of troubadours, truly kind and colorful,
Or eighteenth-century marquise, distant in décolleté,
Or celebrated prostitute of our parents's time,
Or, I don't know, something modern—I can't quite conceive what—
All of this, whatever it may be; if it can inspire, let it inspire!
My heart is a dumped-over bucket.
As those who invoke spirits invoke spirits, I invoke
Myself and I find nothing.
I reach the window and see the street with absolute clarity.
I see the stores, I see the sidewalks, I see the passing cars,
I see the living beings, well-dressed, in the intersection,
I see the dogs that also exist,
And all this weighs on me like a condemnation of exile,
And all this is foreign, like everything.)

I lived, studied, loved, and even believed,
And today there's no beggar I don't envy just because he's not me.
I look at the rags and the wounds and the lies of each one,
And I think: maybe you've never lived or studied or loved or believed
(Because it is possible to make a reality of all this without doing
        any of it);
Maybe you just existed, like a lizard with its tail cut off,
And that tail, shorn from the lizard, is stirring.

I did what I didn't know,
And what I could do with me I didn't.
The costume I wore was all wrong.
They took me right away for who I wasn't, and I didn't deny it,
        and I got lost.

When I went to remove the mask,
It was stuck on my face.
When I finally took it off and saw myself in the mirror,
I had aged.
I was drunk, I no longer knew how to put on the costume I hadn't
     taken off.
I threw away the mask and slept in the armoire.
Like a dog tolerated by management
Because it is harmless
And I'll write this story to prove that I'm sublime.

My useless verses with their musical essence,
I wish I found you as something I did,
Rather than always standing in front of the Tobacconist's across
     the street,
Stepping on the feet of the awareness of being,
Like a rug on which a drunk man stumbles
Or a worthless doormat the gypsies stole.

But the Tobacconist came to the door and stood there.
I looked at him with the discomfort of a badly cocked head
And with the discomfort of the misunderstood soul.
He will die and I will die.
He'll leave the shop-sign, and I'll leave verses.
At some point the shop-sign will die too, and so will the verses.
After a certain time, the street where the shop-sign was will die,
And the language in which the verses were written.
Then the spinning planet on which all this took place will die.
On other planets in other systems beings like people
Will continue to write verses and live under things like shop-signs,
Always one thing in front of the other,
Always one thing as useless as the other,
Always the impossible as stupid as the real,
Always the underlying mystery as sure as the surface mystery of sleep,

Always this or that or neither one thing nor the other.
But a man went into the Tobacconist's (to buy tobacco?),
And the plausible reality suddenly dawns on me.
I look energetic, convinced, human,
And I intend to write these verses in which I say otherwise.
I light a cigarette when I think about writing them
And I savor in the cigarette the release of all thoughts.
I follow the smoke as a route of my own,
And I enjoy, in a sensitive and competent moment,
The release of all speculations
And the awareness that metaphysics is a consequence of being in
      a bad mood.

Then I lie back in the chair
And I keep smoking.
As long as Fate allows, I'll keep smoking.

(If I married my laundress's daughter,
Perhaps I'd be happy.)

Given this, I get up from my chair. I go to the window.

The man is leaving the Tobacconist's (putting change in the
      pocket of his pants?).
Oh, I know him: it's Stevens, who is without metaphysics.
(The Tobacconist arrived at the door.)
As if by a divine instinct, Stevens turned and saw me.
He waved goodbye to me; I shouted, *"Goodbye, O Stevens!"*,
      and the universe
Restored me, without ideals or hopes, and the Tobacconist smiled.

Only Nature is Divine

Only Nature is divine, and she is not divine...

If I speak of her as of an entity
it is for to speak of her it is necessary to use the language of men,
which gives personality to things,
and imposes names on things.

But things have neither name nor personality:
they exist, just as the sky is big and the land is wide,
and our hearts are the size of a closed fist...

I am blessed by everything as far as I know.
That is all I truly am.
I enjoy everything as one who is here in the sun.

The Tree of Silence

If our voice grew, where was the tree?
To what ends, the corolla of silence?
Heart already tired, you are the root:
a bird passes you en route to another country.
Earthly things are word.
Sow what is silent.
It doesn't matter who plows,
if you don't reap what you loved.
So, why not take them,
syllable and leaf, in a single bunch
with the graceful roundness of one hand?
(Don't you keep quiet? Don't you keep quiet?!)

The Shell

My house is a shell. Like the mollusks,
I patiently secreted it from me:
tidal facade, a dream and waste,
the garden and the walls are only sand and absence.

My house is me and my whims.
Pride laden with innocence
if sometimes you have a balcony, you win
the salt that crumbles the saints in their niches.

And glass roofs, and fragile staircases
ivy-covered, oh fake bronze!
Fireplace open to the wind, the rooms cold.

My house . . . but that's another story:
It's me in the wind and the rain, here barefoot,
sitting on a stone of memory.

Verses to a Little Goat I Had

With her moist snout
this little goat picks up
any sign of dew on the grass
in the night.

That hanging flower
appeals to her step;
it seems the seed
is her little chime.

Her dark hairs
keep watch on the night;
every hair sensing a drop,
from footsteps, dust, life.

Of silence, briars, hunger,
composed in full udders
the whole reason for her name
and the fruit of her walks.

As she strolls gravely
like ships coming in,
weighed down by the thoughts
of her soft life.

And finally, the pure boulder
of her little tail,
is like the egg and the bird:
big secret,
balanced.

Ship

My flesh is sore
from the landing of some birds
I don't know where they're from.
I only know that they, like life,
sting in my heart.
When they come, they come softly;
leaving, they go so heavy!
How I like to be
here at my window
giving my mind over to the birds!
I'm looking at the sea:
look at that aimless ship!
And, seeing it, give it a lamp,
or my sad eyelashes:
the bird and the ship, in a nutshell,
here, at my window.

Poetic Art

The poetry of the abstract?
Perhaps.
But a little warmth,
the exaltation of each moment.
It is better.

When the wind blows
there is flesh in the breath;
when the fire rises,
that first blaze,
then dies down, something burned.
It is better!
An idea,
only the lifeblood of trouble;
anyway, no,
I don't care.
An idea
is worthy of a promise,
and to promise is to arc
the big arrow.
Just the flank of things bleeding moves me,
and one question is painful
when it opens a breach.
Abstract!
Abstract is always reduction,
dryness.
It loses,
and before me the rising sea is green:
it dips and widens.
So, no:
neither the abstract nor the concrete
are exactly poetry.
Poetry is something else.
Poetry and abstract, no.

Two Poems by Luís Filipe Sarmento

What Is a Poem?

Tell me, pedantic servant of the Europe of executioners,
what is a poem? Tell me, O chameleon of interests
that capture you and throw you into the impotence of being a man
in solidarity, what is a poem? Tell me, humiliated puppet
at the hands of those who bought your soul, body, and lucidity,
what is a poem? Tell me, O sell-out to the obscure aesthetics
of the patriarchs who murder your brothers
and who keep you as an infamous lackey, what is a poem?
Tell me, failed "poet," what your bald ignorance tells me
about what a poem is. Will it be an abstract meal
to be served to the provincial vamps who sponsor you?
Or an American pastiche with a jazz flavor
to camouflage your sinister ideology of human farce?
Tell me, O pretender of grace, what is a poem?
Tell me, O star-struck by the Euro, what is a poem?
You are under pressure from the north and you tell me nothing about
what a poem is. They bought you silence
about death at sea between our lands, our people,
and they gave you empty words so that your "People,"
reeking of alcohol, make verses like one who masturbates
and flatters the brides of power. Tell me, what is a poem?

Take Refuge

Take refuge in your conscience, without crosses or crescents,
without wires or walls, without barbs or hatreds; and you will
     soon recognize
among the crowds of wanderers that permeate your memory
your ancestors from afar who gave birth to you here.
Where do you come from? To which original cave do you belong?
What languages
sail the seas and rivers of your blood? How many gods
did you worship, asking and hoping that the future would not be
     this present?
Where are the divine answers?
Take refuge in your conscience, without the fear that priests
of hidden power want to impose on you nor the anguish of the
     destroyed dream.
Observe the renewal of the sea, the regeneration of the planet,
every unconscious attack of the madman, and you will soon see
the power of the bowels of this magnificent globe,
as if it were a head that thinks the possibility
of defeat is the impossibility of life and makes it reborn
in all its splendor, the colorful map of what we really are:
take refuge in your conscience as host of the future
and do not fear the gods, who are divine and who understand
     each other
far from this Earth, and open the doors of your humble hovel
as if it were a palace against death
and against the chaotic image of the end.

Two Poems by Sophia de Mello Breyner Andresen

25th of April

This is the dawn I expected—
the first day, whole and clean,
where we emerge from the night and the silence.
And free, we inhabit the substance of time

Discovery

An ocean of green muscles
An idol with as many arms as an octopus
Incorruptible chaos that erupts
And orderly turmoil
Dancer twisted up
Around the outstretched ships

We cross rows of horses
Who shake their manes at the trade winds

The sea suddenly became too young and too old
To show the beaches
And a people
Of newly created men still clay-colored
Still naked, still dazzled

From *The Calligraphy of Birds* by Ângela de Almeida

let us start the day in the east by the ravines
with our hands enfolded in rings of water
and look at the blue satin blanket
and let us stay absorbed and free
and suspended
and with our hands enfolded in rings of water
let us simply embrace each other
and continue to look at the blue satin blanket
as if time were this moment
so smooth and astonished
and in the end, let's not embrace, but simply
look at the trickle of water on the skin
of this different day and stay like this
contemplative and absorbed
while the water flows and never dies

   —for Ricardo Reis

Villanelle on a Line Hated by Auden

"We must love one another or die,"
 The poet instructs, though doesn't believe it.
"We must love one another and die,"

 Revised to inclusive *and* on another try,
 Then repudiated the poem, banning it.
 He who must love another or die.

"Ours is not to reason why,"
 Another poet said with the soul of wit.
 Ours is to love one another. We die.

 Changing a word makes meaning fly
 To the far reaches of our minds and sit.
 Must we, really, love one another or die?

 Can we exist without knowing why—
 Knowledge straining at the bit—
 Until we can only love each other and die?

 When we live without love, we die.
 At least, those of us who desire it.
 We must love one another or die.
 We must love one another and die.

A Cento dei Cantos di Ezra Pound

What thou lovest well remains,

                     the rest is dross

a man on whom the sun has gone down

and the wind came as hamadryas under the sun-beat.

What thou lov'st well shall not be reft from thee

nor is it for nothing that the chrysalids mate in the air

              color di luce,

green splendor and as the sun through pale fingers.

What thou lovest well is thy true heritage—

I don't know how humanity stands it

        with a painted paradise at the end of it

        without a painted paradise at the end of it

the dwarf morning-glory twines round the grass blade

        whose world, or mine or theirs

                or is it of none?

       Nothing matters but the quality

of the affection—

in the end—that has carved the trace in the mind;

dove sta memoria?

Pull down thy vanity, I say pull down.

The mountain and shut garden of pear trees in flower

here rested.

What thou lovest well remains—

from *Fallow Field*

I

Fallow Field

The old car is there,
where she left it,
out by the old shed,
breeding rust—obscured
from the roadway by the rye grass
that grows up all around.
Long triangular tentacles
blowing and bending
in the hot breeze, as
sunlight filters
through gathering clouds.
By now the grass has worked
up into the engine block.
The car
is planted now,
in this fallow field,
awaiting bulldozers.
They call this grass
"poverty grain," and there's
no small comfort in the fact
that it's as tolerant
of poor soils
as she was of her marriage.
On the day she left,
she packed her whole life
into an old grip: clothing,
framed photographs
of the children, her parents,

the salt cellar she'd bought
on her honeymoon in Rome.
While packing, she'd given
pause that her whole life
had become so
portable, where once there'd
been permanence. And now,
she blows and bends—
rye grass on a midsummer afternoon.

Naming

The way a name lingers in the snow
when traced by hand.
The way angels are made in snow,
all body down,
arms moving from side to ear to side to ear—
a whisper, a pause;
slight, melting hesitation—

The pause in the hand as it moves
over a name carved in black granite.
The *Chuck, Chuck, Chuck,*
of great-tailed grackles
at southern coastal marshes,
or the way magpies repeat,
         Meg, Meg, Meg—

The way the rib cage of a whale
resembles the architecture of I. M. Pei.
The way two names on a page
separated by thousands of lines,
pages, bookshelves, miles, can be connected.
The way wind hums through cordgrass;
rain on bluestem, on mesquite—

The sandpiper's tremble
as it skitters over tidal mudflats,
tracking names in the wet silt,
silt that has been building
since Foreman lost to Ali,
since Troy fell—building until
we forget names altogether—

The way children, who know only
syllables endlessly repeated,
connect one moment to the next
humming, humming, humming—
The way magpies connect branches
into thickets for their nesting—

Curve of thumb caressing
the letters of a loved one's name
on the printed page, connecting
each letter with a trace of oil
from fingerprint to fingerprint,
again and again and again—

Black Angus, Winter

I

The angus rap their noses
on the ice—
fat, gentle fists
rooting water
from the trough.
They kick up clods of dirt
as a madrigal of shudders
ripples their hides.

II

The barn needs painting,
it's chipped like ice
from an ice-cutter's axe.
The fence also needs work,
posts leaning, wire slack.
The Angus keep still—
they're smarter than we think,
know all about electricity.

III

I cross the barnyard
on my way back from the pond,
ice skates keeping time
against the small of my back.
The sting of the air
is tempered by the heat of manure.
Through the barn door:
Veal calf jabbing at her mother's udder.

Deserted Sheep

Lambs, jostled, *forgive*
    the wolf, break
    its taste in lamb
into a toddler's gallop,
bumping headlong

into thick-piled ewes—
lanolin slicking their noses, as
they stumble on the fescue
dotting the valley,
a pointillist's landscape.

No shepherd, no sheep dog,
no gate to enter; a small,
orange plastic snow fence,
neatly staked at four corners
with steel posts,
gives form to the sheepcote.

The last ounce of sun
a violet tremor *the wolf*
    forgives, lingering
along the western ridge,
    the shepherd's fear
returning to the valley.

A ram, brown and flocculent,
secures a silent corner
of the fold—eyes intent
upon a slow-moving shadow.

Granite

"All night the eyes of deer shine for an instant..."
—Kenneth Rexroth

Cleansed by burns, their headpieces
have outrageous symmetry.
Snow bunting at the birdfeeder: Alighting,
knocked-away by nervous sparrows
two birch stands from the hillside.

Splitting wood,
as trees shift their shadows
in the weight of winter.
It's easy to get lost in these woods,
yet be sure of design.
As eyes of deer vanish into the feldspar,
muscles aching, sweat soaking shirt.

The oak door to the yellow house
opens with a louder noise
than that with which it shuts,
belying its hundred years.
And inside, the hearth is tested,
faces, around the granite,
recognized for their hypnotic gestures.

In the house, stamp down the day.
Snow from boots
melts on the granite firebreak.
The deer don't notice
when you've gone.

Dead Red Wing

Of your famous epaulets
only a hint
on the shoulder,
           like a wound
opened when my
finger luffs the down,
still dappled with immaturity.
Tangy scar from thorn or thicket,
but not the end of you.

Come spring, you'd be up
in the low trees,
on telephone wires,
bowing foxtail in the marsh,
your song become vain:—
"Look-at-meeee . . . Look-at-meeee . . . "
Flash of red on black wing
poised to singe the eyes
trained on you,
a life-bird,
through field glasses.

In my hand you are stiff,
unrecognizable.
The woman
who brought you
to the birding group
kept you
in a Ziploc bag
in the freezer,
next to the roast
and last week's red beans.

Every evening,
when she finished her vigil
at the window,
she took you out,
rubbed your cold breast,
ruffled feathers,
sang your song.

Confusing Fall Warblers

"You changed your name from Brown to Jones and mine
from Brown to Blue..."
—George Jones

Was it Hank Williams
she called the Nashville warbler,
or was it the black-throated blue?
Was it Wilson's warbler
she heard in the bog up north
chattering *chi chi chi chi chi chet chet?*

Yellow-throat or orange-crowned,
from Tennessee, Connecticut, or
Canada, the prothonotary
clerks for the vireo from Philly,
who is neither lawyer nor warbler,
but is often mistaken—

Was it the hooded warbler
that startled her from the thicket,
or mourning warbler's balancing notes
chirry chirry, chorry chorry,
that made her cock her head
to listen for its secret?

And tell me, tell me truly,
was it only
that sad country song
playing on the car radio
that made her cry?

—after Roger Tory Peterson's *A Field Guide to the Birds*, plate 52

Spartina

Herring gull dragged from the cord grass by a feral, bay cat,
who drops the sputtering gull under a tree.

The gull's left wing and leg are broken—right wing thrashing,
body turning round a point, compass tracing a circle.

Wild chorus of gulls tracing the same circle in salt haze
only wider, concentric, thirty feet overhead.

The cat lying down in shade, making furtive stabs,
powerful paws slapping down motion.

The cat's feral, calico-covered muscles ebb and shudder
in the bay breeze, waving in wind and water.

Now she yawns indelicately, fur and feathers
lofting on the incoming tide.

The gull plants his beak in the sand,
tethered, like all of us, to fate.

Gleanings

OCEAN GROVE, NEW JERSEY

Look at the two of them, bent
to the early morning tide.
Culling glass from the gritty surf.
Strange and wonderful alchemists,
who search for the elusive blue
of medicine bottles, caressing
emerald imitators from "Old Latrobe,"
or amber sea urchins
left there like whelks at low tide.

They discard broken bits of crockery,
forsaken jetsam of the sands.
Beach glass is opaque
with a false clarity:
Polished by sand and sea,
the edges don't cut
like our lives, lived elsewhere,
out beyond the last sandbar,
where plate tectonics rule the waves.

—for Diane Stiglich & James Supplee

Hope Against Hope

My mind is a slate gray sky about to open up over the capitol.
Electricity grounds itself to Rhode Island's terminal moraine,
and Narragansett Bay is alive with activity.
Providence is like a tree, grafted to increase yield:
the scion of this hybrid is *Freedom* and the stock, *Hope*.
Did Roger Williams have this in mind, on the day
he was expelled from Massachusetts Bay Colony
and exiled to "Rogue's Island?"

My mind is bent to the future
like a fly buzzing against a table lamp,
guided by some unknown power to the light.
Spruce-trees freckle Rhode Island's low hills,
like "Indians" on horseback overlooking a settlement
in some old western. *Years are not a life,*
trees come down with heavy snow or summer storms,
others are cut to fuel fires in cast-iron stoves,
or are cleared for houses on subdivided acres.

Providence is an article of faith
as much as of divinity. Maybe a life is determined
in the balance of past, present, and future.
Providence, in the immutable language of trees:
Tulip-trees heavy-laden with their "magnolia" blossoms;
post oaks, twisted and stunted, like worried warriors;
ash, hickory, hope; willow, red spruce, blood;
poplar, pine, providence; sandy loam, eelgrass, freedom;
arrow-arum, water weed, Wampanoag; hope against hope.

Salt

Blood, leached of redness,
in a confluence of tears.

Sweat of a lover,
in evaporating recline.

Dry bones and breath
—the taste of dreaming.

Sargassum drifting
in a pelagic wave.

Body in Motion

Sinew, charge, and light—
muscle etching a concourse of air,
heat and flutter
thrum of pump house,
or pop of ligaments
snapping shut.
So quiet the fabric of skin,
taut, slack then taut again.
Flex and stretch with single purpose,
gauge of weight and distribution.
Placement of form becoming new,
as in never accomplished before,
as in a position to be named later.
Sublime, the arc of breath:
ether of air, atom, matter—
particles colluding in space.

Saudade

"I feel beliefs that I do not hold. I am ravished by passions I repudiate."
—Fernando Pessoa

We're surrounded by people
who sentimentalize collegiate life,
swoon over first marriages,
or live in days gone by.
The Portuguese have a word for it,
saudade, a longing for lost things.

For myself, I have fond memories
of houses in New England
(where my childhood
blossomed, disappeared);
of a life of the mind.

But what I long for
is the old cherry tree,
in front of our home
—we were newly wed—
how it dashed its branches
against our roof.

Opportunity

A wasp wrestles all day
with the false freedom
of a windowpane.

Scaling the glass, then slipping
down, buzzing the cracked paint
of the old window frame.

As if thrumming wings faster
will pull it closer to the blossom,
just beyond its reach.

So determined in its struggle
to get in, to wrest pollen from
the exotic flower on the other side.

A spider sets its dinner table
in the corner of the pane—

Day of the Earth, Night of the Locusts

Owlspent, our days are numbered,
we count them in their passing
with eyes closed, and night comes
easily to those who sleep
with blinded eyes wide open.
And double-talk is all we get
from those whose hands hold fate.

In the larkspur
at the grove's end,
pagan by rite,
we suss the folly of symbolism
and awaken
to the owl's haunting.

Eyespeak, our gods implore us
to look beyond our smugness.
And there, we find
our temples
are burdened by wreckage
and our own misdeeds.

Do we good justice by our actions?
Uneducated stewards, electable
guardians of a lackluster paradise.
The apples bruise to the grasses,
blades fat as a night-sweat.
The others have little say,
our own descent is a cant—

The question is:
Can we be faithful stewards
when there is no bounty?

Two Views

*"Ya know, I wouldn't fall a tree with them in it. But I sure like to tell
them that. I just get lippy. I get fired up . . . you tell them anything."*
—Arlington Earl "A. E." Ammons

I

How tall you are,
longer than my life here
among these blades and oil.
Felled, you might be half
the length of a football field,
yet I can't get inside of you.
Somewhere in there
past the cambium,
is a beam so straight
it could support my two kids
about to enter college.
    Dead-standing,
you're a condo complex
for invertebrates.
Heartwood shipped overseas,
waste wood pulped
then glued together again,
you'll make a sturdy chair.
You are mine. Without me,
you are nothing; I made you useful.
If I leave you, you too will leave.

II

I can hear you breathing,
like hundred–year–old men

who've counted their lives in cigarette packs—
Your phloem constricts,
there are knots in your shoulders
no massage could work out.
My hands are stained guilty
with cadmium red paint, as
I brand the yellow Cats
on their hindquarters,
feed sugar into their gas tanks
to stall their insatiable appetites.
Unlike horses, they don't
nibble my fingers.
We are leveled in leveling you.
You have stood for ages;
no one alive has seen you
in your youth.

The Glimmerglass

being a sequence of stanzas concerning Lake Otsego
("The Glimmerglass"), which forms the headwaters of
the Susquehanna River in Cooperstown, New York

The bats skim
over the evening ripples
of Lake Otsego.
In their blind minds
they see reflection.

❧

The curious mountains
meld with their image
in the looking glass.
In their obvious stillness
they decline comment.

❧

Lime-colored duckweed
splays patterns
on the marsh water,
red sky corn-dancing
on Sydney's Hill.

❧

The sun sets
behind the Webster Farm.
As it falls deeper, clouds pass in the haze.
Speckled cows, curious sheep
freckle the hillside.

ℓ

Freshly harvested,
farmer Webster's hay
will be baled the following day—
the secrets of summer heat,
revealed & thoughtful.

ℓ

The moon rises
from behind the back
of the Sleeping Lion,
turns her face
to the glimmering star.

ℓ

Dark, silent wood
balancing the four corners
of this room—
Through the window,
see the falling water.

ℓ

Long-awaited
tenacity of rain,
giving way to a sun-doused
day of departure.
Farewells, *soaked sleeves*.

The Vermont Quartet

Benj A. Thresher Builds Logging Sleds in Barnet, Vermont

He culls the perfect heartwood from a log,
as if the runners came from grace divined,
each sled he makes will have no analogue.
Some days he longs to hang it all, unwind,
but to his tiresome work he stays inclined.
The sleds he makes seem anxious for the snow,
providing livelihood, or peace of mind
for people in the valley there below.
Toil and trial, he works with little show,
and plies his craft attentive and alone.
In confidence, his workshop light aglow,
he knows a cornmeal pudding waits at home.
When night's etude lends solace to his days,
he'll sleep, preferring pudding to all praise.

Imagining Memphremagog

We've planned to see her every year
since first we heard her dulcet tones:
The serpentine lake with shores of stone,
where French is spoke in rasping hues

and snaps the roofs of frozen mouths,
reminds us she starts in old Quebec.
The rain or wind has kept us south,
and west, in Burlington, or further

outside of Starksboro, *de rigueur.*
It seems a long way, there to here.

But I imagine Memphremagog,
in my mind's own birch bark canoe;

The Abnaki as our guides, we trust
she'll be there on our northward thrust.

The Country of Misgivings

Hermit crabs, we move from place to place
dwelling in other's houses not as guests.
Less welcomed by the owners, face to face,
our lifestyle leaves us timid soloists.
As quickly as we think, we lose perspective,
that gets us into trouble with the law.
So, we discard the house we thought protective;
never learning is our one great tragic flaw.
Blame the country, "Its character is lacking,"
set out by foot or rail to find new lands.
Never think it's our own fault we're sent packing,
without our wits, we fly from other's hands.
Though we may never, ever know the truth,
this country of misgivings begs the proof.

Mt. Mansfield Dilemma

Up near the summit we yield a chance
through nature's own delineation.
To us, at least, a choice that is best:
Autumn behind, winter up ahead.
The brilliant calico valley's grace,
which speaks to us of meals and bed,

or the icy evergreen expanse,
which crops the mountain's bulging chin
and calls into mind my two day face.
From the coy starkmourn of alpine sedge,
we see through Smugglers' Notch up north,
to the feet of whiter mountains east,

or west across Champlain's swirldeep
and blue Adirondack highland's mirth.
Now we pass over the terrace steep,
that spans all this man's field's craggy edge,
and from this place we choose our course:
To return, but not go back to earth.

Reckoning

I

Your abacus of worries,
me, counting my own pace, afraid
of the one real thing
I've known in years—
Negotiating our vertiginous October,
up through birch, maple, oak, cedar, white pine;
granite rising like barnacles on a humpback.
How do you stay calm?
Conceit hangs from my pack
like an extra water bottle.
I have trouble listening:
Do you want to push me over the summit,
or knock me out with a chunk of granite?
The mountain is not mine, I fool myself
when I play the king.

II

We get turned around, tricked by language:
The ring of civilization in "Forest City,"
or the sylvan slur of "Forestry."
The wrong trail is the one I've chosen—
And through the muddle, darkness comes,
and fourteen miles is the double of seven.
We switchback over the mountain's bulge
and bushwhack round its base,
hours multiplied by circumference.

III

At last back at camp,
we learn to count on each other.
From the stone house meadow:
Our prankster's rising hump.
We curse and praise its witchery.
On that rock-ribbed blackberry hill
of Vermont's quiet reckoning, we
calculate the chalk silhouette
in a moonlit night's
heavy charcoal horizon.

Osage Moon

TALLGRASS PRAIRIE, PAWHUSKA, OKLAHOMA

The moon
is a soft pinprick
in a sky
so expansive
even Ursa
Major seems minor.
A dog barks
and ghost voices
echo down Indian song—
piercing the silhouetted Osage hills.
Grasses are weather-worn
and wild; wild-
flowers lie dormant—
everything abides green days.
Besides, cold weather slants
in from the north, taking the plains,
where a few days ago
hot winds came
up from the Gulf of Mexico,
fooling the dogwood,
and fires seared the earth
the color of burnt toast.
Miles, miles of dry grass
and sky
in every direction—
binding grasses,
four-color wildflowers,
and forbs pressed between pages,
tangled in bluestem.

And there, where bison stood
at noon, sheltered
by blackjack oak,
only shadows—
unruly apparitions,
under the Osage moon,
awaiting the culling
of their existence.

    —for Annick Smith

Midnight Sun

AT APPROXIMATELY 59° 43' N LATITUDE, 154° 53' W LONGITUDE

Each night,
I watch the sun set
over Lake Iliamna
through the willows.
How physical,
the names of willows:
Bebb and Scouler,
feltleaf, arctic, undergreen—
names ill-suited for their frail appearance.
And how palpable the story,
told by the black-capped chickadee
about the four bears who come
each night to the village,
linger for a couple of hours,
then vanish.
As the bird now vanishes
from atop the satellite dish
outside the room at Gram's B&B.
He leaves behind
a white remembrance,
which disturbs the signal
coming from Anchorage,
interrupting a program about
the formation of the Hawai'ian Islands,
and sending ripples of multi-colored "snow"
swirling into TV screen volcanoes.
While back outside,
midsummer sun barely sets on the village,
angling over sparse willows
and spruce, bentgrass and sweetgale,

perhaps twinflower, although
verifying the presence of that species
may require a second look.
A second look, which the sun
will suggest, upon its return
four and one-half hours from now.
That is when the BLM surveyors will arrive
on their ATVs (whatever the weather
and whether they're foolish or clever),
to verify yesterday's measurements,
as they do each morning,
in this village of willows
and midnight sun.

An Unkindness of Ravens

ANCHORAGE, ALASKA

To fall asleep at night, I count ravens
from my bedroom window.
They gather in the spruce trees
at the edge of the woods,
as snow gathers dusk on its surface.
By midnight, thirty or forty
have gathered there in the oily dark.

As a group, they are called "an unkindness,"
but they are polite
and helpful to each other,
share their successes and failures
pursue joy and embrace their strength
in numbers, which is more than we can say.

Plummeting downhill, they launch into air,
as if snowboarding; flipping and spinning
—hell-bent teenagers on a half-pipe.
In more sober moments, they tell each other
where to look for food, when danger is near,
and where the good garbage is. They discuss
variable wind speeds or compare moose meat
found in the woods with that of roadside kills.

They can be graceful on the wing—Naiads
of the air—or clumsy and indelicate,
half-eaten bagels dangling from black beaks.
Dusk comes later and later these evenings,
and morning arrives sooner, winter almost over.
Come Easter, the ravens will be gone.
Ravens prefer dead things remain dead.

The Ten-legged Polar Bear

"You Westerners don't understand consensus. You think it means
mutual agreement. Consensus means mutual understanding."
—Gregory Anelon, Sr., Yup'ik elder

Ten legs are better than two
only if they work together—

when all five legs on one side
and all five legs on the other side

move in concert like a sled runner,
the Qupqugiaq moves smoothly,

but if the legs get tangled up
and one leg trips up another,

then another trips another,
the whole bear comes crashing

down; it takes a lot to get
a ten-legged polar bear upright

and get it moving again—

Hoarfrost and Rime

Hoarfrost and rime will soon embrace
devil's club, spruce, and kinnikinic,
sharpening autumn colors in fading light.
Now the last blueberries, overlooked
by dozing bears, await Raven's bidding;
now tundra swans gabble and *woo-ga-loo*,
as the sun lowers its angle over river and tundra,
over those of us who call the "Great Land" home.

Disappearance

In the distance we see what appears to be floating sea-ice,
calved from ragged ice-edge, only it's rounded, tensile, mammalian—

Hollow points of light emanating from softly echoing,
transparent follicles; then a broad back surfaces, inanimate—

"Oh my god, it's a bear!" someone shouts, pointing
to a floating carcass now seen clearly: not sea-ice,

but sea-*bear*—*Ursus maritimus*—dead-man's floating
miles and miles from the nearest shore,

face staring deep beneath the surface, massive front paws
spent from stretching, from reaching for ice-edge,

exhausted from swimming panicky circles,
finding only heavy arctic seawater, viscous oil, adrenaline ooze.

Think of a fight-weary heavyweight, no longer at the top of his game,
up against a nimble, invisible opponent, now down for the count.

   —for Jasper

III

Bread

*"Christ may have risen all at once, the gospel according to Betty
Crocker seems to say, but flour and yeast and people made of dust
require successive chances to reach their stature."*
—Garret Keizer

He takes the bread from the oven, pausing
midway between the bread board and cooling rack,
absorbing the gluteny scent through crusty skin
—the color of a child's arm
after a long hike on a summer's day.

His friend says, "I'll bring you a marvelous sourdough starter,
passed on to me from a cousin who ran a bakery—"
One pinch of starter travels two-thousand miles,
five hours through adventure, through altitude.
"It makes bread that Jesus would be proud to call body."

"Just a pinch?" she asks. "How can you deny me?"
She says that not to let her test it is tantamount to lack of love.
He gives in, just to see her face grow sanguine and lustful.

He once baked thirteen loaves for a homeless shelter;
then, nervous over numerology, he baked a fourteenth.
He couldn't remember which one had been the offending loaf,
so, he started all over again. This time he scored each one
with a distinguishing mark using the blade of a sharp knife.

In the bread bowl, he mixes flour, water, salt.
Kneads, lets it ferment. Kneads again, pulling and folding,
folding and pulling, lets it come into fullness.

Then lifts it into the oven, from where it will emerge
so finely crusted, so evenly textured, so giving of itself.
Bread that cries, when placed in her mouth,
"Eat me and you will never die."

—for Mark Augustus Herrera

Intelligent Design

The knee is proof:
there's no such thing
as "intelligent design."
If there were, the knee
would be much improved,
rather than in need
of replacement.
The doctor tells me
they are doing
wonderful things
with technology these days,
have improved the joint
and bond—
Amazing, really, they
can take a sheep's tendon
and attach it there and here
or remove ligaments
from one part of the body,
secure it by drilling holes
and plugging them up,
stretching until taut
with tension superior
to the original.
The new designs
are so much better
("my better is better
than your better")
it seems obvious
the Creator
took off the afternoon
to play a round of golf
leaving the joint between

thigh bone and shin
to an intern.
Isn't it *obvious?*
I mean, two million years
of evolution haven't
improved the knee one whit.
Nothing intelligent about it.

Second Skin: A Sestina

In the yard by the barn was a snake
resting on a leaf-pile in the garden,
nearby his old shod skin
limp and lifeless under a noon-day sun.
Abandoned on the blades of grass,
like an untangled filament of memory.

The sight of him fired my memory,
which cast a shadow on the snake
(who now slithered away in the grass).
He lent a curious aspect to the garden—
aspect being its relation to the sun
—not unlike *his* relation to the skin.

He seemed to remember the skin.
(Do snakes *have* that much memory?)
Or was it a trick of the sun
that he mistook for a female snake?
When he made his way out of the garden,
I crept along quietly in the grass.

As I followed him there in the grass,
he stretched ever closer to the skin;
his path leading out of the garden,
as if tracing the line of a memory.
How strange, I thought, this snake,
disregarding the late summer sun.

Later, over-heated in afternoon sun,
I lay down to rest on the grass.
I watched again as the snake
tried to resuscitate his discarded skin,
perhaps to revive its dead memory
and lure it back home to the garden.

Cutting the lawn by the garden,
I must have been dizzy with sun,
or dozing in the haze of a memory.
Translucent flakes feathered the grass:
it was then I remembered the skin;
it was then I remembered the snake.

I sat by the garden dropping fresh-cut grass
onto my arm and its sunbaked skin,
clippings of memory snaking through my mind.

Redbud and Pitbull

The mining bees are emerging.
Males zipping around
tiny holes in the ground
where females are burrowing
beneath the redbud.
The males have a curious display;
more manic than romantic,
expecting a mate to think crazy
is sexy or superior.

I guess we all
fall prey
to a little crazy love
now and again,
do something foolish,
cross a line or two.
But the bees flying too close
to the ground are just frantic,
I can't imagine they'd make
suitable mates.

They course and dive and zip
(yes, that's the best word for it, *zip*),
while females wait below the redbud.
My pitbull Calvin watches
the mining bees swirling
above, around, and into the ground
beneath the redbud. He thinks,
Who or what are these (things)
buzzing and drilling in the dirt?

Truth is, the mining bees
—neither food nor friend—
pay him little interest.
Now Calvin grows bored,
slopes over to the sidewalk
flopping down in the sun.
The redbud's waxy leaves
glisten in the same sun,
green edging into red.

Calvin is mottled, piebald,
brindle and white with a big brown
eye patch that makes people smile.
He's a lover, not a fighter.
He cares little why the redbud's shock
of fuscia flowers, like scales or
a rash running up the limbs, hasn't shown.
He has no word for flowers
and little time for bees.

Calvin's Story

"Make it stop, make it stop,"
was all I kept thinking;
my eyes closed, some
bully biting my body, limbs,
tearing flesh and hair—
Boys pinned me to the pavement,
each one holding a leg, holding
me down on my back.
Another boy—so there were five?
—pressing the bully into me
head lashing at anything
it could grab with canines.
I'm surprised I didn't black out—
Then, I remember a scuffle.
I was almost unconscious,
drifting in an out—
Two men freed my limbs,
but still I couldn't move.
One chased the boys
while the other lifted me,
cradled me, into a van.
I'll never forget the smell
camphor, maybe, almost
lavender, medicinal.
The gentle one dabbed my
wounds with a wet cloth,
stroked me slowly, dabbed
—there was a lot of blood;
were there sirens? I don't
remember sirens. (Should
there have been sirens?)

The next thing I remember
is being on a cold, metal
table—a nurse or doctor
looking me over—another
shaking her head. The first
mumbles something (all I hear
is "Dog," that word they have
for us), then I'm sure she said,
"This one's a keeper, let's give
him a second chance..."
I wake in a crate, damp towel
beneath me, head swirling.
I must be in the "pound,"
there are others barking.
(I wish they would be quiet;
my head hurts.) Then
the pretty nurse or doctor
comes in, mumbles to me;
I look up, try to smile
(this seems to please her),
and I slip in and out of sleep.
                    Months later,
I'm sitting on a street corner,
leashed, with some of the nice pound
people. A lot of people pass by,
they pat my head, mumble
in that way they do, until one
couple lingers (a child or two
are with them, I can't recall).
They mumble to the pound people;
one of them (Alpha, I'll call him)
walks me; he has a firm hand,
but is gentle, in control.

Oh, how I wish for a forever
family . . . but I don't
want to get my hopes up.
Then, the day is over,
back to the pound—sigh—
guess it wasn't meant to be.
Next night, however, there
is Alpha, and he's brought
some others. (Oh, let me be
on best behavior so they will
take me home.) They seem
to like when I snuggle, listen,
take commands, lick the cute
young ones—they are salty sweet!
Days go by after that night,
the pound people tell me
to get ready. Maybe, just maybe,
this is a good sign. Oh, I get so
excited my butt wiggles faster and
faster. Finally, the day comes;
Alpha arrives with the others,
and I think, *This is it.* I'm going home
with my forever family . . . to a home;
home at last for my second chance.

Passion

Devoid of passion, life's a mockery, really.
Like Shackleton's crew deprived of carbohydrates
surviving only on seal meat and penguin
those many months shipwrecked
in their quest for crossing over the frozen continent.
Yet we swim in it every day. Hours drag;
no one breathes or forgets to breathe.
The net drags the unfrozen river,
but the bodies are cold, cold—
Are they frozen? Are we frozen?
We fall on our assets, as the fortunes fall.
We remain timid, perhaps a little gun shy.
Opportunities are lost at every turn.
We cannot dive in for fear of getting—
Of getting what? Caught in the ice?
A broken leg or heart? The fracture will only
set if you let go; thaw comes only with friction.
What exactly are you waiting for?
Action is the basis of success.
As for passion, it can't be reasoned; only negotiated.
I'm digging in my heals; think there may be
a wire coming across explaining,
only no one knows the sender.

Listen, listen—*LISTEN!*

Firestorm

He sees the firestorm run across
her forehead like a lightning bolt
in 3D, and he knows she is going
to her dark place.

He rubs his thumb along that spot
where they say the 3rd eye
is found, and she looks at him
wondering how he knows.

They wait for the rain to stop
refill their coffee cups for
the 3rd time, not ready to leave,
knowing they can't yet stay—

He texts her from across the table.
It's the 3rd word that will stop her,
target of all his desire. He smiles
as the emoticon returns to her face.

Risks Are Risky

"Risks are risky; waiting is painful, indecision worse. If your
heart tells you something, take it, relax and enjoy."
—Paulo Coelho

Risks are risky, stasis is static.
No one ever moved forward
who did not take a first step.
As we risk, we grow,
some would argue,
others would never leave
the house—too risky.
Ah, but the rewards—so sweet.
Risk is a probability
of specific eventualities,
resulting in an impact,
beneficial or adverse.
From the Arabic, *"rizk,"*
meaning "to seek prosperity,"
risk has inherent volatility
and unexpected variables.
It could be worse—
"Love is reckless," wrote Rumi.
"Reason seeks a profit."
Should we risk it all,
take a gamble, commit:
What gains! What possible returns!
Or hold back, cut loose at our stop-limit?
But what if it is the one opportunity,
the one investment that keeps giving;
that we have waited for all our lives?
We cannot know. But uncertainty
is risky too. The uncharted river
flows we know not where.

The river leads us onward,
but how can we know
what is around the bend:
oxbow or waterfall?
Or confluence: where two streams
come together to form a new river.
Even derivatives derive from *something*—
Whether in matters of romance or finance:
Risks are risky, but prosperity is thriving.

The Financial Suicides

Damned and damning are the fools,
their bald heads forgetful of sins.
Believing greed and graft are virtues,
they made all the rules,
spent lavishly on short-term views,
and made off with the most wins.

Masters of the Universe,
they excel at immoderation, going all-out,
but mastered neither failure nor humility.
Faced with losing everything or worse—
riches and status—they take the tidy,
albeit cowardly way out.

In the end, they come to find out
everything that man builds or begins
endures only for a moment.
Their legacies, without a doubt,
are consumed in the fires they foment
with their lies, deceit, and sins.

IV

(Section IV of *Fallow Field*, omitted here, consisted of poems from *Dwelling: an ecopoem*, published in its entirety by Shanti Arts, 2018.)

V

The Poet Gene

The gene for "poet" has likely been isolated,
somewhere in a lab in southern California.
And I wonder how close it is to the gene
that makes you crave potato chips
or the "coffee-drinker" gene, perhaps,
or the one that causes procrastination.
If they have the poet gene cornered
in a Petri dish, will they admonish it
for all the bad poems ever written,
however unwittingly?

Would it improve the human
to have the poet gene spliced
into fruit or beef—or even bacon?
Poetry-enhanced bacon. Now *that's*
genetic modification one can get behind!

What if this innocent experiment turned wicked?
Oh, but what if it went "aft agley"?
Think of it, more bad poems by more bad poets—
(Increased productivity isn't always a good thing.)
Perhaps *this* poem is, in fact, one of them,
a mutated, altered, monster poem
waiting to grab you by the throat and . . . *Ahem.*

Think of the sheer volume of bad poetry
overtaking the world, smothering us;

entire forests decimated for paper
upon which these poems are printed
or hundreds of iPhone apps built
to accommodate a staggering number of poems
cranked out by "GMPs" (genetically modified poets)
careering and MFA-ing all over the place.

Undoubtedly, someone will decide to splice
the poet gene from one poet into another. Then what?
Talk about trouble: one side striving for simplicity;
the other deliberately obtuse and indirect.

No, best leave the poet gene out of even this poem;
rather, focus on how to make potato chip consumption
actually slimming to the human figure, especially
when consumed with large quantities of your favorite ale
and generous servings of bacon.

The Postlude, or How I Became a Poet

"What dwelling shall receive me?... The earth is all before me."
—Wordsworth, "The Prelude"

I am a child, crawling around in the leaves
With Gladys Taylor while she names the trees,
Parts the grasses, digs into the earth with a gardener's trowel.
She picks out worms and slugs, millipedes
And springtails, which we see with a "Berlese funnel."
Busy decomposers working their busy tasks,
Turning waste into energy, leaf litter into soil again.
Gladys names things for me: "That oak,
That maple there, that sassafras, smell its roots."
                    "Root beer!" I exclaim,
Her laughter peeling away into the hills. Later,
With Comstock's *Handbook of Nature Study*
On the table next to the unending jigsaw puzzle,
Gladys opens to "The Oaks," reading or reciting:
"The symbol of strength since man first gazed
Upon its noble proportions ... " Then she sings Virgil,

        Full in the midst of his own strength he stands
        Stretching his brawny arms and leafy hands,
        His shade protects the plains, his head the hills commands.

Leaves and acorns spread across the table,
Each divided to its source, as if cataloguing specimens:
The white and chestnut oaks, red and scarlet,
Every oak in the neighborhood, sketching the leaves,
Tracing and coloring them. Then questions, such questions:
"Where did we see this one growing?" "How tall?"
"Are the branches crooked or straight?"
"Round leaves or pointy?"
                    And then a game of matching

Acorn to leaf; a most difficult lesson—as difficult
As those jigsaw puzzles for a boy lacking patience
Or attention. Outdoors again, to *learn* attention,
Naming the birds that came to eat at the feeder:
Chickadee, sparrow, nuthatch, tufted titmouse,
The ubiquitous jay.

                "The mockingbird, hear
How he makes fun of all the other birds." Now
Thrasher, now robin, the *sweet sweet sweet*,
Very merry cheer of the song sparrow,
Or the flicker's *whicka whicka wick-a-wick*.
Then a jay's piercing caw, a cat's meow,
This was all the mocker's doing! And wide-eyed,
I stare, as Gladys seems to call birds to her side.
"The robin tells us when it's going to rain,
Not just when spring is come," she says. "Look
How he sings as he waits for worms to surface."

           That summer, rowing around the pond
By Brookfield's floating bridge, I saw a beaver
Slap the water with its tail, and then swim around the boat,
As if in warning. Under water a moment later he went,
Only to appear twenty yards away, scrambling up the bank,
Back to his busy work. *"Busy as a beaver,"* Gladys laughs.
Then a serious tone, "You know that beavers gathered
The mud with which the earth was made?"
(I later learned this was Indian legend; to her
There was little difference among the ways of knowing.)
All around the pond the beavers made of the creek,
The sharp points of their handiwork: birches broken
For succulent shoots, twigs, leaves, and bark bared.
"When they hear running water, they've just got
To get back to work!" Beavers moving across
The water, noses up, branches in their teeth,

Building or repairing dams or adding to their lodges,
Lodges that look like huts Indians might have used.

I watched for them—beavers and Indians—when
Out on the water, and once I remember a beaver
Jumping clear out of the water over the bow of the rowboat!
Later, wading in the mud shallows by the pond's pebbly edge,
I came out of the water to find leeches covering my feet,
Filling the spaces between my toes. Screaming, fascinated,
I learned that they sucked blood, little bloodsuckers,
A kind of worm, which were once used to reduce fever.

That was me to Gladys Taylor's teaching,
Wanting to soak up everything she had to give me.
We picked pea pods out of the garden, shelled
On the spot, our thumbs a sort prying-spoon,
And ate blackberries by the bushel or bellyful,
Probably blueberries, too, I don't know. And
Seeing the milkweed grown fat with its milk,
I popped it open, squirting the white viscous
Juice at my brother. Gladys always found
A caterpillar on the milkweed leaves, tiger stripes
Of black, white, and yellow. "Monarchs," she said,
"The most beautiful butterfly you'll ever see."
I looked incredulously at the caterpillar, believing,
Because she was Gladys, but not believing her,
That this wiggly, worm-like thing could be a butterfly.
Later, she found a chrysalis and took the leaf
And twig from which it hung. She placed it atop
A jar on the picnic table, and each day we waited
—waited for what? I didn't know. Until one day,
It was empty, a hollow, blue-green emerald shell,
And I almost cried. "Look, out in the meadow,"
She instructed. Hundreds, it seemed like

Thousands, of monarch butterflies flitting about,
From flower to flower!
                              The wooly-bear
Was easier to study. We put it in a jar with a twig
And fresh grass every day; it curled and slept and ate
Until one day it climbed, climbed to the top
Of the twig and spun a cocoon from its own hairs.
There it stayed for weeks, until at last I thought it dead.
But then, emerging from its silky capsule, a hideous sight:
Gray, tawny, dull—a tiger moth! Nothing like the cute
And fuzzy reddish-brown and black teddy bear we'd found.
"This is magic," said Gladys. "*Nature's magic.*"

And I believed her, believe her still, that there is some magic
In nature speaking within us when we are in it, *of it*, let it in—
Science may explain this all away, physics or biology,
But nothing will shake my faith in this:
That the force of nature, the inner fire, *anima mundi*,
Gaia, or whatever you may call it, is alive within each
Being and everything with which we share this earth.

    My Mother Earth was Gladys Taylor, and she
Taught me these things, and about poetry and art,
In the few, brief years we had together. Gladys
Taught me how to look at the world—to pay attention.
Thus began my education from Nature's bosom:
A woman, childless herself (I believe) who,
In her dungarees and work-shirt, took a child
Under her wing and gave him *gold*,
Gave him his desire for dwelling on this earth.

—in memory of Gladys Taylor, November 17, 1902–January 1, 1986

from *30-Day Poems*

I awake at 4:30 a.m.
to the sound of a bird
I can't identify by song.
He teases me from inside
the magnolia just off our deck.
In the pre-dawn light,
I can't spot him among the buds.
I think of Issa:
"Singing since morning
Skylark, your throat
is parched." Climbing back into bed,
I see you sleeping.
So beautiful in the early light.
My happiness is anything
but average.

ɕ

Hard night rain . . .
Morning departure:
Soaked sleeves.

.

My love exits the train,
making her connection
—shapely legs.

.

Magnolia blossoms
soaking my sleeves,
wet with longing.

.

Four days too long.
but then—
what time is enough?

ح

1:30 a.m. Can't sleep.
I don't like when we fight,
especially via text, and
especially about being apart,
which neither of us enjoys.
I distract myself with old movies
on TCM, and try to forget
there's still two days to go.
Even Selznick's "Since You
Went Away," can't take me away,
with its sentiment and sorrow,
and the hint of a sappy ending.

Back story: Jennifer Jones,
whose affair with Selznick led
to her husband Robert Walker's breakdown,
plays a teen (at 25) having to pretend
she's in love with her ex-husband,
not with her director.
Joseph Cotton's Virginia
gentleman not sinister at all,
showing his range as well as
his limitations. My limitations
stare me in the face
from the screen—
and from this empty bottle.
While you steam and fume
and try to sleep, 100 miles north.

ԑ

When I saw your familiar face
in the picture I painted almost 30 years ago,
I understood Frost's delight
and "surprise of remembering
something I didn't know I knew."
Same feeling of recognition
overtook me when twice we met before.
What was it I recognized?
"Something I didn't know I knew,"
became something I didn't know
I needed in my life, and then
something I couldn't live without
in every dream, every night, and every day.

ԑ

Last night's full moon
appeared further away
than usual, reminding me
that it is moving away
from us an inch and a half
every year. Its pull
stretches us thin
and complicates our emotions.
The "pink" moon angles
through our window
and across our white
sheets. Your tangle
of red hair on the pillow
reflects tiny lights
neither high nor low,

as if your dreams
escape into the night.

&

Love is never perfect
and neither are you or me.
You don't walk on water;
I prefer to swim under.
There is nothing
over my eyes, neither
gauzy nor hued.
I see your flaws
and raise them with mine.
And I love you
even in your imperfections,
which I won't enumerate here.
And even with all mine. (Ditto.)
That's real love, baby.
Get used to it. It's yours
if you want it—

&

"Freedom's just another word for nothing left to lose..."
goes that old Kris Kristofferson song.
But we lose something
every day, free or chained—
cells, skin, hair, memories.
Time goes too, the sparrows
mark it outside our window,
mourning doves coo
and whisper, their throats
parted by morning mist.

We rise slowly on mornings
we're alone together;
our bed reluctantly loosing its grip.
"I ache to be in your hold,"
you wrote in a dream.
My poetess of sleep.

&

That's an unattached male
mockingbird who sings
at 3 a.m., hidden somewhere
in the magnolia behind our
building. He wants a mate.
I've got a mate, lying next to me,
and she rolls over and remarks
about the bird, asks why
he is singing now, before dawn.
It's a strategy mockers have developed,
taking advantage of silence,
as if in competition with the night.
Waiting will not do for the mocker,
who has already stolen other birds'
songs, he now wants to win
a heart of his own—
what he doesn't realize: his singing's
as annoying to the females
as it is to us trying to sleep.

ℰ

Breakfast on our deck in the morning sun:
spinach-feta-egg-white omelet,
the last of the rosemary bread toasted,
French-pressed coffee, the *Times*.
Proving to ourselves at least,
civilized life can continue,
even with the hoard of kids
(the smallest perfect number)
looming in their beds.

ℰ

I wanted to kill that mockingbird
this morning, with his incessant trilling,
which would have caused excitement,
and made our morning a tad more thrilling.
My love held close to me in the kitchen,
as we were making breakfast,
her curves beautifully accentuated
by her tight-fitting nightgown.
The kettle whistled, as did I,
when she looked at me so longingly,
and curved her body up to mine.
Ah, if only we had the time
this morning, but the month has come
to an end. Tomorrow we begin again,
but with no less poetry in our lives.

Uncollected Poems

Shepherd

You prepare a table for us
in front of our enemies,
picking the sheepfold clean
with your own hands—
raw with the sting of nettle,
stained the color of sheep laurel.
Your back is stiff from bending,
filling your crooked arm
with false hellebore—
to keep us from having
one-eyed lambs—and lupine.
From the bluestem foothills
comes the hush of rustling.
You look to the north,
sighting down landscape,
scenting the wind.
Your breath fills air,
pungent as pipe smoke.
Goodness and mercy, friend,
come forth from you as naturally
as clouds darkening this valley.
We would follow you anywhere,
dear shepherd, putting fears aside,
although you often seem foolhardy
in this green land, this restful pool.

    —after Psalm 23

Spring Storm

The rain comes with the familiar cadence
of an old friend chattering-on
about nothing in particular.
And the still, small voice
comes from out of nowhere
—an unlikely sound in a spring storm.
No thunder, no trumpet:
"So this is your house and how you keep it."
The house, lived in for years,
perhaps recently swept clean
—I keep a house fit for spiders.

And the still, small voice that resonates
below thunder, comes with a calm,
moves like an undulance in a pine floor,
reaching under the rain
to take part in the holy chorus,
encircling in a pool of slow-moving glory.
We talk about redemption,
talk about the need for the personal,
and then go quietly about our work.
When the storm ends,
it's with a murmur, "Peace be with you."

Sing praises, now, for that stillness
and for the need to make out the sound;
sing praises, now, for the thunder,
which did not come with the rain,
but that filled our hearts
of a spring evening, in our repose.
It is our own voices calling to us,
and we must take heed.

More than Peace

Peace takes many forms:
wholeness, fullness, and completion;
integrity, healing, and harmony;
loving and being loved; forgiveness and reconciliation;
a ceasing of fire, of strife, of anxiety.
Peace is not just an absence of war,
it is also being safe from fear.
A tuneful sound—*shalom*—is to be in harmony,
in well-being, restored in right relationship:
human to God, God to human.

Yet peace, which we all strive for,
eludes us and can seem ever distant.
Although we all share one simple rule,
"Do unto others as you would have done unto you,"
we end up doing unto others as we would never
have done unto us, we rarely love our neighbors
as ourselves, we let refugees wash up on shore
ignore their entreaties with our refusal,
and elect people who ignore commandments
they think don't apply to them.

Still, we are human, we do the best we can.
We are capable of great pity, empathy, resistance.
Shalom means more than peace:
it means we still have a chance, as long as we breathe,
to seek peace in others and ourselves.
Tranquility is an act of persistence,
soundness of a bell in tune
ringing throughout all our days.
Even as mountains fall and hills shake,
righteousness and peace shall kiss each other.

    —for Sasha

Blended Family

When families are blended
it's not like a smoothie,
where all the ingredients
combine to make a new flavor.
In the multi-flavored family,
each flavor remains unique,
each name remains its own.

There is joy in blending families,
but sometimes tears, too.
You don't deny the one for
the other, you are more
together, yet equal apart.
You are "and" rather than "or."
There is more of you—

So, praise our blended family,
let it bring abundance into all our lives.
Let there be strength in our numbers,
as there are now more shoulders
to lean on, more hands to lend,
more hearts to be kept in,
more love to share in its union and bond.

And let each of us
make the best that is all of us
shine more brightly, now, together.

The Narrowest of Margins

Narrow, as in "narrow escape,"
as in "just in the nick of time,"
as in the long thin line
between being caught and going free.
Rattle of train wheels on
thin rails. Metal on metal.
Mettle or margin?
Margin, as in the edges prescribed,
as in the space between,
as in the blank stare of the innocent.
Trapped in a plot she can't escape.
Torn between being who she is
and who they want her to be.
"A fortune if they seal her lips,
a bullet if they fail..."

And the guy? He just wants to
escape himself, but he can't—
The time-worn "get justice for my partner"
card carries his day. He has to do
his job, his "rotten detail."
He must carry out the plan,
which incidentally shifts with every
twist, every jolt of the train—
wheels on rails, metal on metal—
testing his mettle.
On this "night train heading west,
loaded with Suspense."
Death riding the rails
and the long thin line disappearing
into the narrowest of margins.

—for Joanne Leva

The Cartographer's Gambit

In the spindrift,
he outlines an island
for which there are no visas—
whose mapping is all too delectable,
whose charting is measured intensity.

Along these shores,
he conjures ochre bluffs, which resemble
well-turned ankles, the cleft of breast in a covescape,
and hillsides of amber light.
These are things he brought to life on paper, restless for rescue.

The uncharted territory
still gleaming in his eye—
a coastal mystery.
He lumbers, cools with the injection.
The seaboard nearly finished, dry land
his last frontier.

He reads Celine as open waters dry,
the cold spring chills him, he smokes a cigarette.
Deep within his blood, a fine line beckons—
with perfect geography.
Outside, the air is perfumed,
with a scent of powder.

Starlings prattle above him,
black, iridescent, oxymoronic:
a thousand triangles
of gun metal
fusing a jade sky.
Their opacity blinds him to reason.

Unable to move latitudinal or long,
he measures the scale of possibility,
sights his compass on true north and,
as the needle riddles the vein,
he dashes the coast with blue.

—in memory of Peter T. Boyle, 1952–1989

The Quaker Graveyard in Plymouth Meeting

"The Lord survives the rainbow of His will."
—Robert Lowell

A field of marble and granite boulders,
Grave markers of long dead Friends;
Their stones sunk in the ground or sinking,
Becoming one with the earth—
"Coulston," "Skeen," and "Livesey";
"Tomlinson," "Webster," and "Foulke."

My eye is caught by a pinwheel spinning
Propped up by a fresh-cut stone:
The grave of a toddler, named
For a tree that weeps.
Her gifts too early left this Earth;
Her body returned too soon.

—in memory of Willow Ann Donaldson,
August 5, 2007–December 27, 2008

The Other Half of the Sky

Whether gray, cloud-covered or sapphire-clear blue,
embraced by the rosy fingers of Dawn,
or ablaze with a fiery sun going down,
mirrored in the sea along a rocky shore
or contrasting in her brilliance,
the other half of the sky
leads with empathy and grace
always growing, changing, challenging
herself and those others around her.
If you can keep up with her—
a kite aloft, fluttering in her wind—
you are in for the ride of your life.
If you can catch her—
a butterfly dancing, flower to flower—
you must let go of her precious life.

A outra metade do céu

Seja cinzento, coberto de nuvens ou azul safira-claro,
abraçado pelos dedos cor-de-rosa de Dawn,
ou em chamas com um sol ardente a pôr-se,
espelhado no mar ao longo de uma costa rochosa
ou contrastantes no seu brilhantismo,
a outra metade do céu
lidera com empatia e graça
sempre crescendo, mudando, desafiando
ela própria e os outros que a rodeiam.
Se conseguir acompanhá-la—
um papagaio no ar, tremulando-se em seu vento—
estás na boleia da tua vida.
Se conseguir apanhá-la—
uma borboleta a dançar, flor a flor—
deve largar a sua preciosa vida.

translated into Portuguese by Scott Edward Anderson

My Friend Finch

My friend Finch visits me each Tuesday,
when he knows I ought to write a poem,
telling his stories in an illuminated way.
A Samaritan, he once worked for Home-
land Security, designed surveillance
systems to guard against terrorists;
now, a person of interest, helping freelance
in a way that, by and large, consists
of violent measures ably performed
by three friends, Mr. Reese, Fusco, and Shaw.
And then there's Root; she's a nut-job, informed
by the system he created, a flaw.
Still, if I'm in danger or threat mortal,
I only hope it's Finch who gets the call.

> —for Don Paterson, inspired by his "House" &
> after "Person of Interest"

Crow's Rosary

Hoboken again after so long gone, yet the gregarious scent of
    coffee lingers;
the *ka-chung, ka-choong* of the old furnaces is replaced by the
    dolorous
buttoning of starched white collars—

Tinderbox matchbooks, this town harbors a legacy of fire—
a last-resort for some to stem the tide of condo-conversion.
The siren-scourge filling the air once filled by shipyard steam.

One crow equals one square mile in this mile-square-city and
    that lone crow
follows me from rooftop to steeple, from apartment to train depot,

end to end and back again—*"Carrion waiting, carrion waiting!"*
    he cawcries.
Somewhere on the cobblestone Court Street, he stops—
the garbage piled high in the alleyway.

Resuming flight, his feathers soiled by ashes, carrion of this
melting pot boiling over too high a flame—his rosary chanted-out above
the rooftops; church bells echo the litany of the displaced, "Carry
    on waiting."

"I'll die in your rosary," sighs the Hoboken muse. "So carry on waiting."
The Hoboken muse, the wife, dressed in black even in the heat of summer,
soothes the dusky sky.

The hammer's hammer harkens: "Make way! Make way for the
    new tide that
rises above the din and dun! A new sleep is upon us!"

No morning comes without the hammers calling for work to be done;
another home displaced in Hoboken. They never cease except for
the obligatory coffee break taken 10 minutes after waking us all up.

A peregrine falcon rests on our laundry pole out back,
starling-eyed—showing us the underside of our breadwinning days,
challenging us to use those drear, found things.

The litany of lonesomeness leaves nothing left for the crow's rosary
to be counted on. In the weepdusk, he cries in a deafening crowd,
"Carry on waiting, carrion. Carrion waiting!"

The curry-garlic-jalapeno-covered walls and streets now come
prepackaged, processed for microwaves and barbecues—

I see, in my eros-dreaminess, your suppliant flesh
resting on the tar beach; feel the embrace that comes
when our flesh conjugates a verb—

while the crow, soaring alone, surveys the tumult of our
        disheveled days.
This is a ghost of Hoboken—and I am to carry on with my waiting,
carry on as the crow with his lonesome rosary.

Who has the time to let the coffee steep, to savor the "last drop"?
And what does this new Hoboken mean to us, so unlike what it
        was to us?

Altar-clouds rise above us, an endless stream of
forgetting and rising, forgetting and rising,
linked by the crow's rosary, the litany of lonesomeness.

There's a gibbous moon out back, illuminating the night kitchen.
"Thee sees we love our garden," says the Hoboken muse. "Let me
      assure you:
tho' it may be only clapboards and clay pots now, its future is
      arborous bounty . . . "

We live in shells cast aside by others, hollow bodies awaiting
      obsolescence.
Knowing this, the streets seem more calamitous.
Knowing this, we set about preparing the earth's redeeming.

Now you come to me with your chalice of hopelessness:
We are never so alone as when we long for lost things.

32 Facts about the Number Thirty-Two

1.   32 is envious of "33" because it is surrounded by mystery on the back of a Rolling Rock beer bottle.

2.   32 is the smallest number n with exactly 7 solutions to the equation [Phi] $\varphi(x) = n$.

3.   The Curtiss T-32 Condor II was a 1930s American biplane and bomber aircraft built by the Curtiss Aeroplane & Motor Company and used by the U.S. Army Air Corps for executive transport.

4.   Year 32 (XXXII) was a leap year.

5.   Jesus is said to have been crucified in Year 32. (Was that BC or AD? I can never remember.)

6.   The country code "32" is for Belgium. (You could call Hercule Poirot, if he wasn't a fictional character.)

7.   32 is the new 23.

8.   32 is the number of piano sonatas by Beethoven, completed and numbered.

9.   32 degrees is the freezing point of water at sea level in Fahrenheit. In Celsius, 32 degrees would be approximately 90 degrees Fahrenheit.

10.   Apparently, there are 32 Kabalistic Paths of Wisdom. (I wonder which one Madonna is on?)

11. 32 is the atomic number of the chemical element germanium (Ge), which is to say 32 is the number of protons found in the nucleus of its atom.

12. 32 is the number of teeth in a full set of an adult human if the wisdom teeth have not been extracted. (If you are without wisdom, you are said to be foolish or full of folly or not playing with a full deck [of teeth?].)

13. 32-bit is the size of a databus in bits.

14. The Route 32 bus in Philadelphia will take you from Roxborough to Center City.

15. 32 is the number of pages in the average comic book, excluding the cover wrap.

16. Number 32 is for Shaquille O'Neal, Kevin McHale, Karl Malone, Magic Johnson, Dr. J, Sandy Koufax, Steve Carlton, Claude Lemieux, Marcus Allen, Jim Brown, and Franco Harris. (It is no longer for OJ Simpson, for reasons that don't belong in this poem.)

17. There are 32 traditional counties in Ireland, which were formed between the late 1190s and 1607.

18. "Thirty-two Short Films about Glenn Gould" is a film about the Canadian pianist Glenn Gould. The film is, as the title implies, divided into thirty-two short films, thereby mimicking the thirty-two-part structure of Bach's "Goldberg Variations," a recording of which Gould made famous or which made Gould famous, I'm never sure which came first.

19. The thirty-two-bar form, often called "AABA" from the order in which its melodies occur, is a popular song form, especially among Tin Pan Alley songwriters and in rock & roll.

20. "Deuce Coupe" is a slang term referring to the 1932 Ford coupe. "Little Deuce Coupe" was a pop song written in the 32-bar form by The Beach Boys.

21. In the thirty-two-bar form, the musical structure of each chorus is made up of four eight-bar sections, hence 32 bars.

22. Some yogis believe there are 32 bars of energy running through our heads storing the electromagnetic component of all the thoughts, ideas, attitudes, decisions, and beliefs that we have ever had about anything.

23. It was said that there were once 32 bars in Hoboken, New Jersey, a city of one square mile.

24. "Thirty-two Kilos" is a controversial series of photographs by Ivonne Thein, in which she altered images of regular-sized models to make them look extremely anorexic, as if they weighed only 32 kilos (70 lbs.).

25. According to the Urban Dictionary, "b-thirty-two" is one of the most dangerous and rapidly growing gangs in Bensonhurst, Brooklyn, and originally started on Bay 32nd St.

26. I have had a 32-inch waist since 1982.

27. By pregnancy week 32, a baby weighs 3.75 pounds and is about 16.7 inches long.

28. Nobody ever says "32-skidoo," although it scans better than "23-skidoo" and it can be used as an antonym for that phrase, which was one of the first mass-popular slang phrases.

29. Psalm 32 begins "Blessed is he whose transgressions are forgiven, whose sins are covered." (Not sure what they are covered with, but that may point back to #16.)

30. Title 32 of the U.S. Code outlines the role of the National Guard and allows members of the Guard to serve as law enforcement in their respective states.

31. A beheaded body can make 32 steps, according to a legend involving King Ludwig of Bavaria in 1336.

32. According to Microsoft Word, this poem is divided into 32 paragraphs, although poetic form dictates, and I would prefer, they be called stanzas.

NOTES

[18] "Wine-Dark Sea"
Some lines, phrases, concepts, and/or details in this poem derive, in whole or in part, from the following sources:

Caroline Alexander, "A Winelike Sea," *Lapham's Quarterly*, July 2013. http://www.laphamsquarterly.org/sea/winelike-sea

Austin Carr, "The Cruise Ship Suicides," *Bloomberg Businessweek*, December 30, 2020. http://www.bloomberg. com/features/2020-cruise-ship-suicides

Euripides, *Bacchae and Other Plays* (Penguin Classics, 2006).

Daphne Hogstrom and Art Seiden, *Paul Bunyan and Babe the Blue Ox,* (Racine: Whitman Pub. Co., 1967).

Homer, *The Iliad* (Penguin Classics, 1998); *The Odyssey* (New York: Vintage Books USA, 2007).

Henry George Liddell and Robert Scott, *Liddell and Scott's Greek-English Lexicon* (Simon Wallenburg Press, 2007).

Maria Michela Sassi, "The Sea Was Never Blue," *Aeon*, June 30, 2021. http://aeon.co/essays/can-we-hope-to-understand-how-the-greeks-saw-their-world

Pedro Da Silveira, *Poems in Absentia & Poems from the Island and the World* (Bellis Azorica), bilingual edition (Tagus Press, 2019); translation: "I look at the sea. I look at the sky. Both blue." (translation by George Monteiro)

Paul Skallas, "Homer's 'Wine-Dark Sea' FAQ." *Medium*, June 29, 2018. http://www.medium.com/@skallasp/homers-wine-dark-sea-faq-15004acbccca

Wikipedia contributors, "Wine-Dark Sea (Homer)," *Wikipedia*, June 22, 2021. http://www.en.wikipedia.org/wiki/Wine-dark_sea_(Homer)

John Noble Wilford, "Homer's Sea: Wine Dark?" *The New York Times*, December 20, 1983. http://www.nytimes.com/1983/12/20/science/homer-s-sea-wine-dark.html

Emily Wilson, "Dr. Emily Wilson on Wine-dark Sea," *Twitter*, January 1, 2018. http://www.twitter.com/EmilyRCWilson/status/948030121415454722

[42] "Prayer House"
A *Masǧid* or *Masjid* (pl. masajid) (Arabic: مسجد—pronounced: /mas.gʲid/ or /mas.dʒid/) is one of two Arabic terms for a mosque, originally taken from the Persian, *Mazgat*, the place of worship for Zoroastrians. The word *masjid* is widely preferred over mosque by many Muslims.

[100] "A Cento dei Cantos di Ezra Pound"
Composed of lines from "The Pisan Cantos" by Ezra Pound; specifically, Cantos LXXIV, LXXVI, LXXXI. "Hamadryas" may refer to Hamadryas (mythology), the daughter of Oreios and mother of the Hamadryads in Greek mythology, or to *Hamadryas argentea* (also called Silvery Buttercup), a species of plant in the Ranunculaceae family. *Dove sta memoria* may be translated "where memory lives" or "where are your memories?"

[133] "The Ten-legged Polar Bear"
Qupqugiaq: a legendary ten-legged polar bear described by the
Inupiaq of Alaska's North Slope.

[161] "30-Day Poems"
These poems were part of a series of poems written over the
month of April 2013, one poem per day, meant to be a quick sketch
of whatever was occupying me at the time. The entire series was
posted daily on my poetry blog: seapoetry.wordpress.com

[162]
"My happiness is anything / but average" is a reference to Issa's
poem:

目出度さもちう位也おらが春
(medetasa mo chû kurai nari oraga haru)

My "Happy New Year!"
about average
my spring

I first became interested in and engaged with Japanese poetry
in the early to middle 1980s through Gary Snyder and Kenneth
Rexroth. I was drawn specifically to the *Man'yōshū* (*Ten Thousand
Leaves* anthology) poets. I liked that the *Man'yōshū* poets were
less well known than the great Haiku poets—Basho, Busan, and
Issa—and that their forms and styles were more varied, including
long poems (*chōka*), short poems (*tanka*), and even short
connected poems (*tan-renga*).

The phrase "soaked sleeves" or "soaking sleeves" was used to
represent tears shed for an absent lover—whether lost or just
far from one's side. It could also connote longing for place or
countryside. I first used the phrase and a loose tanka form in my

sequence of poems "The Glimmerglass," which was written during the summer of 1985 in Cooperstown, New York, and which first appeared in *Terrain* and subsequently, in my book *Fallow Field*. [See pp. 121–122 of current volume.]

[164]
April's full moon is known as the Pink Moon. This name came from the herb moss pink, or wild ground phlox, which is one of the earliest widespread flowers of spring. Other names for this month's celestial body include the Full Sprouting Grass Moon, the Egg Moon, and among coastal tribes in eastern North America, it was called the Fish Moon because it came at the time the shad swam upstream to spawn.

[167]
Beginning with the number 1, if you ADD the powers of 2, and IF the SUM is a PRIME number, then you get a PERFECT number by multiplying this sum to the LAST power of 2. For example, if you add 1+2, the sum is 3, a PRIME number. This means 3 x 2 = 6 is a perfect number. In fact, it is the "smallest perfect number." (My wife, Samantha, and I have six kids between us in our blended family.)

[188] "32 Facts about the Number Thirty-Two"
Derived from http://en.wikipedia.org/wiki/32_(number) and other sources

ACKNOWLEDGMENTS

Grateful acknowledgment to the editors of the publications in which the following poems originally appeared, sometimes in earlier versions:

Abyss & Apex: "An 'Unkindness' of Ravens"

Alaska Quarterly Review: "Naming"

American Poetry Review: "Deaths of the Poets"; "Owl in the Gloaming"; and "Intelligent Design"

American Studies Over_Seas: "Wine-Dark Sea"

A New Song: "Spring Storm"

Anon: "Midnight Sun"

Blueline: "Dead Red Wing"; "Fallow Field"; and "Opportunity"

Building Socialism: World Multilingual Poetry from the Revolutionary Poets Brigade: "Two Poems by Luís Filipe Sarmento"

Chalk Circle: "Crow's Rosary"

Cimarron Review: "Villanesca"

The Cortland Review: "Osage Moon"

Earth's Daughters: "Bread"

The Esthetic Apostle: "Cândido Rondon Remembering Teddy Roosevelt"

Gávea-Brown—A Bilingual Journal of Portuguese-North American Letters and Studies: "Five Poems by Vitorino Nemésio"

Harrisburg Review: "Body in Motion"

Isotope: "Confusing Fall Warblers"

Kimera: "Saudade" and "Salt"

La Petite Zine: "Two Views" and "Hoarfrost & Rime"

Mulher—Coração da Liberdade (anthology): "The Other Half of the Sky/A outra metade do céu"

The Nebraska Review: "Black Angus, Winter"; "Deserted Sheep"; and "Granite"

OCHO: "Village, Batanta Island"

One Art: "Phase Change"

Pessoa Plural: "Two Poems by Fernando Pessoa" (translations) and "Saudade"

Philadelphia Stories: "Spartina"

Picaroon Poetry: "Ant Logic"

Piedmont Literary Review: "The Vermont Quartet"

Pine Hills Review: "Weather"

Poetic Mind Set: "Second Skin: A Sestina"

Referential Magazine: "App to the Stars" and "Love at Middle Age"

Schuylkill Valley Journal: "Prayer House" and "Rice Paddies, Rain"

SLANT: "Sirens Rising"

Terrain: A Journal of the Built and Natural Environments: "Ten-Legged Polar Bear"; "Day of the Earth, Night of the Locusts"; and "Hope Against Hope"

The Wayfarer: "The Pre-dawn Song of the Pearly-eyed Thrasher" and "Under the Linden's Spell"

Zoomorphic: "Doubting Finches"

Several of the poems in the "New Poems & Translations" section were written during Jo Bell's "52 Project," a year-long series of prompts in the 52 weeks between January 1, 2014 and January 1, 2015. (And, yes, I wrote in each week of that year!)

Fallow Field was originally published in 2013 by Aldrich Press, an imprint of Kelsay Books.

"Second Skin" appeared in *The Incredible Sestina Anthology*, published by Write Bloody Publishing, 2013.

"The Poet Gene" received an honorable mention in the 2011 ESRC Genomics Forum Poetry Competition co-sponsored by the Economic and Social Research Council's Genomics Network and the Scottish Poetry Library of Edinburgh.

"Calvin's Story" and "Redbud & Pitbull" appeared in the anthology *Dogs Singing: A Tribute*, published by Salmon Poetry, 2010.

"Black Angus, Winter," "Deserted Sheep," and "Granite" won the Nebraska Review Award, 1997.

"Gleanings" appeared in the anthology *Under a Gull's Wing: Poems & Photographs of the Jersey Shore*, published by Down the Shore Press, 1997.

"A Pantoum for Aceh" was translated into Tamil by Appadurai Muttulingam and published in the Tamil-language magazine, *Uraiyadal*.

"Sirens Rising" was translated into Italian by Francesco Durante and published in *Almanacco Caprese*.

"30-day Poems" originally appeared on the author's poetry blog, seapoetry.wordpress.com, as part of a month-long celebration of National Poetry Month in April 2013.

"32 Facts about the Number Thirty-Two," originally appeared on the back cover of *32 Poems*.

Poets don't write in a vacuum; we are part of a community. While I am bound to forget someone here—and hope they will forgive me if I do—there are numerous people I want to thank and recognize for their thoughts, suggestions, chastisement, encouragement, edits, inspiration, and camaraderie. They include Onésimo T. Almeida, L.L. Barkat, Erin Belieu, Jo Bell (and the "52" group of writers), Diniz Borges (and other members of the Cagarro Colloquium), L.M. Browning, Esmeralda Cabral, A.V. Christie, Alfred Corn, Alison Hawthorne Deming, Anne Dubuisson, John Fleming, Vamberto Freitas, Margarida Vale de Gato, Ona Gritz, Lara Gularte, Donald Hall, Thomas V. Hartman, Robert Hass, Mark Augustus Herrera, Colette Inez, Elizabeth Kaplan, Mary Karr, Karen Kelsay, Lee Kravitz, Jack Langerak, Joanne Leva, Thomas Lux, Kathryn Miles, Daniel Nester, Walter Pavlich, Penny Perkins, Robert Pinsky, João Pedro Porto, Jack Ricchiuto, Andrea Ross, Luís Filipe Sarmento, Daniel Simpson, David Simpson, Gary Snyder, Karen Swenson, and Richard Taddeo. And to my editor and publisher Christine Cote at Shanti Arts for believing my work deserving of a wider audience. And to Kathy Fagan, Christopher Merrill, and Derek Sheffield for their words in support of this book. My wife and life partner, Samantha, has been instrumental in my journey to find my purpose and pursue the path that I am on and that we are on together. Finally, our kids—all six of them in our "perfect number" blended brood—have inspired me and continue to inspire me as a writer, a father, and as a man.
—SEA, January 2022

About the Author

Elena Ray, 2021

Scott Edward Anderson is an award-winning poet, memoirist, essayist, and translator. He is the author of *Azorean Suite: A poem of the moment/Suite Açoriana: Um poema do momento* (Letras Lavadas, 2020); *Falling Up: A Memoir of Second Chances* (Homebound Publications, 2019), which received the 1st Literary Award of Letras Lavadas in conjunction with PEN Açores; the Nautilus Award-winning *Dwelling: an ecopoem* (Shanti Arts, 2018); as well as *Fallow Field* (Aldrich Press, 2013); and *Walks in Nature's Empire* (The Countryman Press, 1995). He has been a Concordia Fellow at the Millay Colony for the Arts and received the Nebraska Review Award and Aldrich Emerging Poets Award. His work has appeared in the *American Poetry Review, Alaska Quarterly Review, Cimarron Review, The Cortland Review, Many Mountains Moving, Terrain*, and the anthologies *Dogs Singing* (Salmon Poetry, 2011) and *The Incredible Sestina Anthology* (Write Bloody, 2013), among other publications.

—scottedwardanderson.com

—@greenskeptic on Twitter and Instagram

SHANTI ARTS

NATURE • ART • SPIRIT

Please visit us online
to browse our entire book catalog,
including poetry collections and fiction,
books on travel, nature, healing, art,
photography, and more.

Also take a look at our highly regarded art
and literary journal, *Still Point Arts Quarterly*,
which may be downloaded for free.

www.shantiarts.com